SPIRITUAL
WARFARE

SPIRITUAL WARFARE

RICHARD ING

![Whitaker House]

Unless otherwise indicated, all Scripture quotations are taken
from the King James Version (KJV) of the Bible.

Scripture quotations marked (NIV) are from the Holy Bible, *New
International Version*, © 1973, 1978, 1984 by the International
Bible Society. Used by permission.

Scripture quotations marked (AMP) are from the *Amplified Bible,
New Testament,* ©1954, 1958, 1987, by the Lockman
Foundation, and are used by permission; or are from the
Amplified Bible, Old Testament, © 1962, 1964 by Zondervan
Publishing House, and used by permission.

SPIRITUAL WARFARE

Richard B. W. Ing
Light of the World Missions
P. O. Box 37451
Honolulu, HI 96837

ISBN: 0-88368-385-7
Printed in the United States of America
© 1996 by Whitaker House

Whitaker House
30 Hunt Valley Circle
New Kensington, PA 15068
www.whitakerhouse.com

6 7 8 9 10 11 12 13 14 / 10 09 08 07 06 05 04 03

Contents

Acknowledgments

Many circumstances and individuals contributed to the writing of this book. Above all is the Holy Spirit who guided and showed me many things over a period of twelve years. I thank the Lord for His love and protection, the many saints who consented to have their experiences shared in this manual for all to benefit, and the leaders who contributed to the total understanding of this necessary area of ministry. Pioneers such as Don Basham, Win Worley, Frank and Ida Mae Hammond, Dr. Rebecca Brown, Elaine Lee, Bill Szubritsky, and Howard Pittman, to name a few, gave time and effort to share their knowledge and experiences.

Special thanks to my wife, Beatrice, and my four children who sacrificed many hours and who worked to fill the gaps caused by my absence from family activities while writing this manual. We are fellow laborers in God's kingdom.

Introduction

Not by might, nor by power,
but by my spirit, saith the LORD of hosts.
—Zechariah 4:6

Many churches shy away from the subject of deliverance or casting out demons. Some claim that by talking about the devil, we give him glory. Others are simply afraid of the subject. Still others don't believe in evil spirits or in a personal Satan. Most speak largely out of ignorance and fear.

This manual attempts to dispel unnecessary fear and to create a simple pattern which most Christians can follow. It was originally intended to be a study outline for the saints at Light of the World Missions. As the text grew in volume, we began to realize that the manual would be useful to many churches and, therefore, modified the text to present a broader spectrum of the subject matter. Such a manual really has no end, since God is almost daily adding new knowledge.

Casting out demons is not new to the church— just forgotten. God is restoring deliverance to the body of Christ today, so we need a knowledge of deliverance and spiritual warfare.

One night several years ago, three elders approached me with the news that God had appointed me the teacher of the church. "Well, God hasn't said anything to me" I replied. The next morning, as I knelt to pray, I suddenly had a vision. I found myself sitting in the last row in an auditorium filled with soldiers in combat uniforms. I saw myself walk down the aisle to the front and then stand behind a podium. Three men were standing to my left. Suddenly, I heard a voice say, "Son, I've called you to teach my army." Since then, God has confirmed my calling many times through various prophets and visions.

At the time, I was already deeply involved in the deliverance ministry. My wife and I often cast out demons and healed the sick—we gained our knowledge through hit and miss, failures as well as successes. God revealed many things to us and we grew by leaps and bounds. It was exciting to see angels and hear the Holy Spirit as He guided us through the battles.

As time went on, we began to read about the experiences of others and were often delighted to find that they had received many identical revelations and insights. We learned much from others in the deliverance ministry. Deliverance is a wave that cannot be stopped because it is of God. It is here to stay. Eleven years ago, I began to teach about spiritual warfare at least three times a week. Eventually, it took me to other churches and countries. In 1990, I put together a manual for use by the local church.

It was an accumulation of the many outlines and sermons I had given in the past. This book is the end result.

Deliverance is not the sum total of the Christian walk. In the end, God will still look at the hearts and reins of men (Ps. 7:9). Love, humility, and truth will always be our standard and goal, but we need to go beyond the foundational principles of Christianity into perfection in Christ.

This book will not perfect you. Only the Holy Spirit can lead you into all truth. But, it will help you in your walk with the Lord. I pray that you will never give up your quest to be like Him.

Chapter One

Can Christians Have Demons?

To deliverance ministers, the question, "Can Christians have demons?" is not even worth pondering. Experiences with thousands of deliverance sessions leave no doubt in my mind that Christians not only can, but do have demons. One famous teacher, Frank Hammond, says, "The question is not whether Christians can have demons, but rather, can I ever find a Christian without a demon?" People stand up during services and declare, "I don't have a demon!" Yet the demon of Pride is manifested all over their faces.

I suspect that most opposition to deliverance comes out of either fear or pride. People who fear demons and the very thought of the devil don't want to be involved. To disguise that fear, they advance an array of doctrines or Scripture to prove either that demons do not exist, or that Christians cannot have them. If their fear is too great, no amount of persuasion will convince them otherwise.

Pride comes in when a denomination or church has officially adopted a "no demons in Christians" stance. It's difficult to change doctrines or positions once you have taken a public stance. No one wants to admit errors in doctrine if it will threaten his reputation. "Face" becomes more important than truth. Occasionally, a church sits on the fence by declaring that Christians cannot have demons but conceding that demons can cling to the outside.

A number of Scriptures are used to support the argument that Christians cannot have demons living in them. Some quote 2 Corinthians 6:14, which says, *"What fellowship hath righteousness with unrighteousness? and what communion hath light with darkness?"* Actually, the Bible does not say it cannot happen. It merely says it should not happen. Jesus supped with publicans, and saints fellowship with unbelievers so that the light can defeat the darkness.

Some saints reason that demons cannot live in the body because it is the temple of the Holy Spirit (1 Cor. 6:19). But we find that the temple in Old Testament days was divided into three main sections: outer court, Holy Place, and Holy of Holies. In Moses' tabernacle, anyone could enter the outer court, even foreigners. The Holy Spirit dwelt in the Holy Place and the Holy of Holies. Similarly, I believe that the Holy Spirit dwells in our spirits or hearts (Eph. 3:17; 2 Pet. 1:19), the demons in our bodies. In Acts 5:3, Peter said to Ananias, *"why hath Satan filled thine heart to lie to the Holy Ghost?"*

In Ezekiel, the prophet dug a hole in the wall of God's temple and found a door through which he entered. He saw *"every form of creeping things, and abominable beasts, and all the idols of the house of Israel, portrayed upon the wall round about"* (Ezek. 8:10). Demons existed in God's temple.

Others claim that when we become Christians, we are cleansed of all demons. The Bible does not say that. It says that our sins are washed away by the blood, but does not mention demons.

It is true, however, that demons cannot "possess" us. Unfortunately, the King James Version of the Bible uses an incorrect word. The correct word in the Greek is "demonization," or having demons. Possession implies total control. Demons cannot possess us, but we can possess demons.

A quick fix for the issue is the contention that demons can only cling on from the outside. However, the Bible does not say that Jesus and the disciples "brushed off," "rubbed off," or "chased away" demons. Instead, the Bible consistently says, "cast out." "Cast out" clearly indicates that demons were "in." To get something out, it has to first be in.

Theological arguments must give way to experience. Even scientists are known to abandon pet theories when actual experiences do not support them. Over 99% of the people I have delivered have been born-again tongue-speaking Christians, including many charismatic pastors. If you do not believe that Christians can have demons, I suggest you attend a number of deliverance sessions. Don't pass judgment until you have investigated the matter thoroughly. It is important to know the truth in these end times. If demons can reside in the human body, then they need to be cast out!

Chapter Two

Satan's Kingdom Exposed

There is a definite progression in the way the Bible exposes Satan's kingdom. I believe this emphasizes the tremendous importance and responsibility given to Christians in the end times to destroy the demonic kingdoms of this world.

The Old Testament reveals very little about demons in the plural. Most references are directed to singular spirits or Satan himself. For instance, Genesis chapter three and Job chapters one and two refer to one serpent or spirit. When Saul rebelled against God's commandments, one evil spirit went to torment him (1 Sam. 16:14, 23). Again, a single lying spirit deceived the four hundred prophets who transgressed against God by prophesying on behalf of Ahab, a sinful king (1 Kings 22:22). There are no indications of a demonic kingdom or hordes of evil spirits.

When Jesus began His ministry, He set free many people who were tormented by demons. He accomplished many of His healings by casting out the spirit of Infirmity (Matt. 4:24; 8:16, 28; 9:33; 12:22; 15:22; Mark 1:27; 3:11; 5:13; 7:26; Luke 4:33, 36; 6:18; 7:21; 8:2; 10:20; 11:14).

Never before had any prophet or man of God cast out demons like Jesus did. His ministry represented a significant departure from anything mentioned in the Old Testament. In fact, the closest thing to deliverance in the Old Testament appears in 1 Samuel 16:23. David played his harp and the evil spirit tormenting Saul departed.

Through the Gadarean incident, Jesus began to show us that: (1) Satan's hordes are almost countless; (2) many demons can inhabit a human body; (3) demons can cause a person to have superhuman physical strength; (4) when a person is infested with foul spirits, many times they cause him to live in foul places or conditions; (5) even though extremely demonized, a person can have cogent and lucid moments; (6) demons can talk back and resist being cast out; (7) demons have intelligence; (8) demons desire to be in a fleshly body, even an animal's; (9) demons fall under a line of authority within geographical limits and are afraid of being in another strongman's territory; (10) demons know the Word of God.

The demons knew what the Word says about the end when they will be consigned to the pit (Rev. 20:1, 3). They also knew Jesus was the Son of God (Mark 5:7).

Overall, Jesus began to reveal our real enemy—Satan and his evil hordes of demons. Never before had man fully understood that the enemy is within.

At the same time, Jesus began to teach how to defeat the enemy. In fact, Jesus specifically announced that He came to set the captives free.

The Spirit of the Lord is upon me, because he hath anointed me to preach the gospel to the poor; he hath sent me to heal the brokenhearted, to preach deliverance to the captives, and recovering of sight to the blind, to set at liberty them that are bruised. (Luke 4:18)

For this purpose the Son of God was manifested, that he might destroy the works of the devil. (1 John 3:8)

Jesus gave his twelve disciples power to cast out demons. He also empowered the seventy to do the same (Matt. 10:1, 8; Mark 6:7; Luke 10:17). He made it clear that all believers should cast out demons. *"These signs shall follow them that believe; In my name shall they cast out devils; they shall speak with new tongues"* (Mark 16:17).

Jesus began to instruct His disciples (and therefore us) how to conduct spiritual warfare. He taught how to bind and loose (Matt. 12:29; 16:19; 18:18; Mark 3:27). He taught how to engage the enemy by closing and tearing down his gates (Matt. 16:18). He taught that evil spirits go to the dry places when cast out, and, if possible, come back with seven more wicked to re-enter (Matt. 12:43; Luke 11:24). Therefore our houses cannot be left empty and ungarnished after the demons are cast out. We have to be filled with the Holy Spirit and the Word. He also gave all believers authority and responsibility to fight (Acts 2:34–35; 1 Cor. 15:25; Heb. 10:12–13).

Jesus' complete victory over Satan's kingdom came through the Cross and His resurrection. He actually spoiled principalities and defeated Satan for us, thereby sealing Satan's fate (Col. 2:15). The demise of Satan's rule is past tense. By the Son's death and resurrection, it was ordained that we are conquerors over Satan's kingdom. The prince of this world is judged (John 16:11). The authority and power to defeat the enemy is a privilege given all His saints. *"Behold, I give unto you power to tread on serpents and scorpions, and over all the power of the enemy: and nothing shall by any means hurt you"* (Luke 10:19). Jesus said, *"The gates of hell shall not prevail against* [the church]" (Matt. 16:18). We are the church.

The book of Acts represents the beginning of further revelation of Satan's kingdom. In several of his letters, Paul referred to principalities, powers, rulers of the darkness of this world, thrones, and dominions.

> *For we wrestle not against flesh and blood, but against principalities, against powers, against the rulers of the darkness of this world, against spiritual wickedness in high places.* (Eph. 6:12)

> *For by him were all things created, that are in heaven, and that are in earth, visible and invisible, whether they be thrones, or dominions, or principalities, or powers: all things were created by him, and for him.* (Col. 1:16)

17

The apostles and believers continued the fight against Satan's kingdom. Peter, Paul, John, and the other apostles engaged the enemy and cast him out.

> *There came also a multitude out of the cities round about unto Jerusalem, bringing sick folks, and them which were vexed with unclean spirits: and they were healed every one.*
>
> (Acts 5:16)

Do you remember the incident when the young girl with the Divination spirit followed Paul and Silas around? They cast the spirit out (Acts 16:18). Casting out demons became so widely practiced by Christians that the Jews attempted to copy them. The sons of Sceva learned a painful lesson when they tried to cast out demons without believing in Jesus Christ (Acts 19:13–16). The man with the evil spirit leaped on them, and they ran away naked and wounded.

If there is one book that all Christians need to study today, it is the book of Revelation. Fifty years after Jesus ascended to the Father, He gave the apostle John a full revelation of Satan's nefarious intention to overcome the saints in the end times that he might rule the whole world (Rev. 12:17; 13:7, 18). Not only that, an encounter between God's people and Satan's hordes will take place. Many of the saints will fall away, and be destroyed, and some will be martyred. But, in the end a remnant of God's people will completely defeat the powers of darkness (Rev. 9:4; 12:11; 14:1–5).

Satan's hordes are well-trained. There is no love among demons—hate and pride rule their actions. But when it comes to destroying mankind, they are united in purpose.

Colossians 2:15 and Ephesians 6:12 tell us that Satan divides his kingdom into principalities, powers, dominions, thrones, and rulers of darkness. This worldwide organization covers every area of the earth. I believe that Satan's highest level of command, called principalities, number at least ten. (Revelation 17 talks about ten crowns, representing ten kingdoms.) It would appear that principalities and dominions refer to areas, while powers and rulers refer to ruling demons. The word "thrones" may refer to the sources of powers.

Satan divides the earth into even smaller areas of control: countries, regions, cities, towns, neighborhoods, homes, churches, families, and individuals. I don't know the exact borders of these areas, but I know they exist.

There is a story of a missionary who was passing out Bible tracts in a town where the main street was the border between Paraguay and Brazil. When he was on the Brazilian side of the street, people accepted the tracts and listened to the Word willingly. When he crossed over to the Paraguayan side, people were hostile and unwilling to listen. Amazingly, he tried to approach one woman in Paraguay, and she utterly refused to listen to or even accept a tract. When she crossed over to Brazil, the missionary followed her. He then offered her the same tract, which she willingly received and then allowed him to preach the Word to her. Later, the missionary learned that the churches in Brazil had been praying and binding up the strongman over their area, but the churches in Paraguay had not. The main street just happened to be the line between principalities.

The Bible says that when Jesus cast out the demons in the Gadarean man, they begged Him not to send them out of the country (Mark 5:10). Demons are extremely jealous of one another and will fight and tear at each other, if given the opportunity. A demon who finds itself out of its assigned area will be subject to attack by other demons.

Strongmen and Ruling Spirits

Satan appoints ruling spirits or strongmen over every principality or control area. The major ones rule from the mid-heavens, and a hierarchy exists in which other ruling spirits control each level in descending order. It ends with a ruling spirit in each individual. It is similar to the chain of command adopted by earthly armies. The generals sit on thrones at the top level while the sergeants at the bottom control the demons that occupy a stronghold in a person.

Demons in the mid-heavens fly back and forth between earth and mid-heaven, or they send messengers. Rulers are large and powerful. Howard Pittman describes many of these demons in his book entitled *Demons—An Eyewitness Account*. Satan considers these huge demons the princes of his kingdom. The strongest represent the highest in rank and so on down the line. Satan rules over his demons by terror. They dare not step out of line, lest Satan declare some horrible punishment upon them. They constantly squabble and vie among themselves, much like humans. Pride and hate abound. Demons absolutely hate Christians.

Connecting Cords

The ruling spirits or strongmen in the heavenlies rule over the spirits on earth. Direct lines or cords between the strongman and the spirits on earth provide spiritual power much like an electrical cord. When battling spirits on earth, you need to bind the strongman over the person or area, and cut and cast off all cords. Jesus says,

> *Verily I say unto you, Whatsoever ye shall bind on earth shall be bound in heaven: and whatsoever ye shall loose on earth shall be loosed in heaven.*　　　　(Matt. 18:18)

Many times demons in a person will act haughty and strong prior to binding up the strongman in the heavenlies and casting off all cords. The same demons became completely frightened and weak when cut off from the strongman. In one case, workers forgot to bind up the strongman, so the demons in a woman resisted and laughed at the workers. "You're too weak for me. You'll never get me out, no way." boasted the spirit. God, however, gave one of the deliverance workers a vision of a large cloud and a small cloud linked together by a cord. The workers recalled that they had forgotten to bind up the strongman and cut off all the cords. Immediately, the spirit whimpered, "Now, why did you have to do that?" It came out within seconds.

Psalm 2:3 says, *"Let us break their bands asunder, and cast away their cords from us."* Psalm 129:4 says, *"The LORD is righteous: he hath cut asunder the cords of the wicked."* Deliverance workers often attest to bands which bind people's minds and bodies in the spirit and cords which connect people's spirits to each other or to the strongman in the heavenlies. Cords are sometimes referred to as ropes or chains around a person also.

Ruling Spirits over Churches

Ruling spirits over smaller areas of control are lower in power, but formidable nevertheless. Satan places ruling spirits or strongmen over particular neighborhoods, families, and individuals. Over a church, Satan may assign Fear, Unbelief, Rebellion, Discord, Pride, Spiritual Death, or some other ruler especially trained to destroy churches.

Churches with heavy discord or dissension may be controlled by the spirits Pride, Witchcraft, Ahab, Jezebel, or Rebellion. Unless they know how to conduct spiritual warfare and bind up the strongman, they will be neutralized by the fighting going on in within the ranks. To some extent, Rebellion exists, or has the potential to, in most churches.

One church I know of had an active congregation of less than 100 families. Members counted thirty-two known cases of terminal cancer. A heavy oppression settled over the church and the spirit Death ruled. Unfortunately, no one there believed in spiritual warfare so Death continued to decimate the membership.

The spirit Unbelief saps a church's strength. It causes people to become lukewarm, so there is little anointing. Unbelief can destroy entire nations. The nation of Israel failed to enter into the promised land because of their unbelief (Heb. 3:19). In spite of many other sins, the writer of Hebrews attributes their failure only to unbelief.

Wickedness in High Places

Revelation seventeen talks about seven heads and ten horns on Satan's beast. Horns represent powers and rulers. Chapter three talks about the seven spirits of God. Since Satan loves to counterfeit almost everything that God does or has, I conjecture that Satan also uses seven or perhaps ten spirits or rulers.

God said to the Israelites:

> *When the LORD thy God shall bring thee into the land whither thou goest to possess it, and hath cast out many nations before thee, the Hittites, and the Girgashites, and the Amorites, and the Canaanites, and the Perizzites, and the Hivites, and the Jebusites, seven nations greater and mightier than thou.* (Deut. 7:1–2)

The trick is to find out what ruling spirit controls your area and then bind it up. Numerous churches report that after binding the strongman over their area, many came to Christ. Dr. Paul Yonggi Cho says that revival came to South Korea after they bound up the strongman. Read his book, *The Fourth Dimension.*

Earthbound Demons

Demons on earth can move very quickly. They range from a few inches to eight feet or more in height. Some appear human, others come in animal shapes or combination of animal and human. Still others appear as shadows or amorphous masses, and a few have shapes beyond description. Many smell terrible.

One particularly powerful spirit takes the form of a half-goat, half-man. From the waist down, he appears as a goat with hooves. From the waist up, he appears as a man. However, his face combines goat and human features. He sometimes wears a vest and eyeglasses. Often, he wears nothing. Greek legends call him Faun or Pan. The Bible calls him Sater or Satyr. In the Hebrew, Sater means Satan. This demon belongs to the group of occultic spirits related to witchcraft and satanism. Very often, he comes down the family line because of occultic involvement by some ancestor. He works with a whole nest of other demons to torment people unfortunate enough to be targeted. He also represents sexual lust.

In Howard Pittman's books *Demons—An Eyewitness Account* and *Placebo*, he describes Greed that rules over the earth during the end times as the average American businessman. I too, have seen this spirit wearing a suit, carrying a briefcase, and constantly looking at his wristwatch.

Sexual perversion spirits assume many grotesque forms, including frog-like shapes, snakes, and scorpions. I have witnessed many manifestations of serpents that cause a person to wriggle, flick his tongue, hiss, and talk like a snake—almost like the serpent in the *Jungle Book* cartoon. These snakes love to wrap themselves around the spine, shoulders, and hearts of men and women. One particular serpent is called "Kundalini." It resides at the base of the spine and is known to adherents of Hinduism.

The spirit of Hades often appears as a large man with the head of a jackal, called Seth or Set. In Egyptian culture, the god of the dead was named Set. Spirits often take on the form of gods and goddesses in Egyptian, Oriental, Greek, Assyrian, and other legends. They love to be worshipped.

Earthbound spirits constantly seek to enter a physical body. These personalities or entities prefer to express themselves in a flesh and blood body. If they cannot stay in a human body, they will seek an animal body. Any body beats none, it seems (Mark 5:13). Evil spirits possess intelligence and emotions far beyond what we can imagine. In the episode of the Gadarean man in the tombs, Jesus asked the spirit, *"What is thy name?"* It answered, *"Legion, for we are many"* (Mark 5:9). A Roman legion consisted of from 2,000 to 10,000 men. Therefore, demonization can involve thousands of spirits dwelling in one person.

Demons Know the Bible

Evil spirits know things men don't. They knew who Jesus was, while the men around Him did not. Demons know the Bible better than you and I. In one episode, a worker misquoted the Bible. The demon immediately corrected the worker and called him "stupid." Early on in my experiences, we called the demons stupid. One worker felt God admonished him by saying, "Don't call demons stupid; they are far more intelligent than mankind." Needless to say, I never call demons stupid anymore. Often, evil spirits will attempt to bribe, reason, or trick you. Without the Holy Spirit, we are no match for demons.

In the Gadarean incident, those demons said, *"Have you come here to torture us before the appointed time?"* (Matt. 8:29 NIV). They knew what the Bible said about their end. They also knew how to reason. When they perceived that they could no longer stay, they asked to be allowed to enter a herd of swine.

Earth bound demons roam everywhere humans do. Some follow people around and try to set up circumstances that will cause a person to fall into sin. Others constantly attempt to enter a person's body and torment from the inside where it is easier to be in control.

Strongholds in Humans

Once demons gain entrance to a human body, they establish various strongholds. For instance, one stronghold may be Infirmity. In such a case the victim is constantly sick and eventually becomes terminally or drastically ill with a myriad of ailments. Another stronghold in the same person could be Unforgiveness, Fear, or Rebellion (their names usually match their functions or jobs).

Within a person, a chain of command controls all strongholds and demons. These ruling spirits and strongholds in a person ultimately take their orders from the strongman in the heavenlies. In order to destroy the stronghold, one must bind up the strongman in the heavenlies, cut and cast off all cords between the strongman and the spirits inside the person, and then continue the deliverance. If you fail to do so, the spirit being cast out will draw strength and reinforcement from the strongman.

Each stronghold represents a nest of spirits, not just a singular spirit. Bitterness may also include Unforgiveness, Hostility, Hatred, Anger, Murder, Violence, et cetera. Hatred could be further separated into Hatred for Father and Hatred for Men. Sexual Uncleanness generally includes Fornication, Adultery, Masturbation, Sexual Fantasies, Perversion, Homosexuality, and other sex related demons.

Temples of the Enemy

Paul says that our bodies are a temple of the Holy Ghost (1 Cor. 6:19). In many cases, evil spirits build spiritual altars or temples in a person because Satan tries to counterfeit every good and holy thing that God has or does.

In one case I handled, a woman from New York took a college class in Hawaiiana, and the course required that the students spend a night in a Hawaiian heiau, or temple enclosure. The students brought tape recorders and video cameras in an attempt to record the presence of Hawaiian spirits. The woman saw nothing, and the only thing that she could remember about the night was having slept soundly on a long rock slab.

Soon thereafter, the twenty-six year old woman began suffering from physical ailments that doctors could not medically explain. During a deliverance session, the Holy Spirit showed me that Hawaiian spirits had an heiau (Hawaiian rock temple) in her body, complete with a sacrificial slab of rock. They planned to sacrifice her by bringing about her death through infirmity. As we tore down the temple gates and walls and applied the blood of Jesus, the demons went berserk. Six people had to hold the woman down on the ground. She tore my shirt, clawed my arms, and spat in my face before the workers could be summoned. My mistake. The spirits fumed as we destroyed the Hawaiian temple and asked God to rain down coals of fire to destroy every element of the temple.

With gods that desire human sacrifice, workers sometimes smell rotting human flesh. With people engaged in Buddhism we often see spiritual temples, prayer altars and boxes, scrolls, incense burners, and other Buddhist paraphernalia in their bodies. Ask God to destroy these strongholds of the enemy.

In one case a woman claimed that Hate and Anger tormented her. As we began praying, the woman assumed a meditation posture. The Holy Spirit revealed that the woman had at one time in her life practiced Buddhism, so an altar and scroll existed in her body. As we destroyed the altar and scroll, the demons screamed, "No! No!"

The worship of other demon gods or goddesses brings similar phenomena. We've come across spiritual temples to the Chinese Kwan Yin, Kwan Dai Goong, and other so-called deities, as well as temples to Indian or Hindu gods and goddesses such as Shiva and Mother Kali. One woman had an altar honoring Diana after she had gone to Greece to worship that goddess. These temples and items exist in the spirit of course.

Demons display an amazing ability to weave myths and legends which encourage worship by foolish humans. Greek, Roman, Chinese, and other legends from innumerable cultures and civilizations show how demons weave stories of romance with conquest. Invariably, these myths feature men who climb up the ladder of immortality with the help of benevolent gods or deities by killing or destroying their enemies. Consequently, men worship special deities in hopes of attaining immortality or at least some hero status. Worship of strange gods and goddesses opens up humans to demon control.

Chapter Three

The Kingdom of Babylon: Jezebel and Ahab

Satan has divided the world into geographical areas over which he has placed ruling spirits or strongmen. These ruler spirits control the spiritual activities within their assigned boundaries.

> When the LORD thy God shall bring thee into the land whither thou goest to possess it, and hath cast out many nations before thee...seven nations greater and mightier than thou. (Deut. 7:1)

God uses the number seven and the expression "*cast out.*" Therefore, it is my opinion that there are seven major powers, although it would seem that the exact number is not material at this time.

The Bible indicates that the seven ruling powers are Jezebel/Ahab, Pride, Witchcraft, Antichrist, Mind Control, Murder/Violence, and Death/Hades.

The influence of these spirits is so widespread that I refer to them as powers as well as ruler spirits. Who can deny that Death, Pride, Murder, and Violence are worldwide powers?

Geographical Areas of Control

Besides these worldwide powers, Satan has assigned specific ruling spirits over geographical areas such as nations and communities, groups such as churches and families, and over every individual. Satan can choose from a wide array of spirits. In a single city alone, one neighborhood could be under the spirit of Poverty, another under Death, and still another under Greed. New York could be under the spirit of Poverty and Death in the Harlem area, Greed in Manhattan, and Witchcraft over the densely Puerto Rican areas.

For groups such as churches, Satan sends Jealousy, Strife, Rebellion, Sedition, Pride, Slumber, and the like. These spirits work hard to bring disunity and failure. Over individuals, he may send Rejection, Hatred, Fear, Infirmity, Death, Cancer, Mind Control, Witchcraft, and a vast array of other spirits calculated to keep the individual from seeking God.

A Plan for Everyone

Satan has a clever plan or scheme for every person, including you. Ephesians 6:11 instructs us to *"Put on the whole armour of God, that ye may be able to stand against the wiles of the devil."* The word "wiles" means "plans," "designs," or "schemes." The devil schemes against you and the body of Christ all the time. Satan's kingdom is not helter-skelter. It is well-organized and has a design to it. What happens on earth is a result of what is in the spiritual realm controlling it. The fruits of Satan's spiritual realm are seen in the affairs of men.

Spiritual Kingdoms

The names of different areas of Satan's kingdom often correspond to physical cities or countries, past or present. Recall the passage in the Bible where the prophet Daniel prayed for twenty-one days before an angel of the Lord came in answer to his prayers. The angel said,

> Fear not, Daniel: for from the first day that thou didst set thine heart to understand, and to chasten thyself before thy God, thy words were heard, and I am come for thy words. But the prince of the kingdom of Persia withstood me one and twenty days. (Dan. 10:12–13)

Who was the prince of Persia? Obviously, it was not an actual human ruler who ruled over physical Persia but a powerful spirit who ruled over spiritual Persia.

In Revelation chapter eleven, the two end-time witnesses of God are killed: "And their dead bodies shall lie in the street of the great city, which spiritually is called Sodom and Egypt, where also our Lord was crucified" (v. 8). We know that Jesus was crucified just outside Jerusalem, so what is this Sodom and Egypt? It is a spiritual city called Sodom and Egypt because its ruling spirits are the same ruling spirits that controlled the physical Sodom and Egypt. Sodom was dominated by every sexual perversion and sin imaginable. Egypt is synonymous with Babylon. Its religion and culture were rooted in Babylon. It was a nation given to idols and worship of the flesh, known for its witchcraft, sorcery, luxurious living, and sexual impurity. Egyptians gods and goddess paralleled those of Babylon, with different names.

The overall satanic spiritual system that encompasses the entire earth is called Babylon the great (Rev. 17:5; 18:2). It is Sodom and Egypt, and much more.

Historical Babylon

Historically, Babylon has long since disappeared from the face of the earth. Therefore, scriptural references to Babylon in the book of Revelation, especially chapters 17 and 18, seem out of place. True, the Iraqi ruler Sadam Hussein has erected a government building where Babylon once stood and has announced plans to rebuild Babylon, but it still remains mostly desert.

The reason we need to discuss historical Babylon is twofold. I believe that the manner in which Babylon was destroyed in the natural reflects how she will be destroyed in the spiritual. Secondly, a study of the culture and religion of ancient Babylon tells us how Babylonian spirits work among us today.

The Destruction

Ancient Babylon was destroyed by Cyrus of Persia around 536 B.C. The city was designed to be impregnable with two huge walls that encompassed the city. These walls were so thick and high that chariot races were held between rows of houses on the tops of the walls. The River Euphrates ran through Babylon and under parts of the walls. The wall contained huge two-leaved gates of brass and iron that resisted attack.

When the Persian army came upon Babylon in the middle of the night, it was surprised to find that the River Euphrates had mysteriously dried up. Nevertheless, the soldiers anticipated a fierce battle at the gates. Lo and behold, when they came upon the main gate, it was torn to pieces, as if some huge hand had ripped it off its hinges. There was no military resistance because the Babylonians had apparently been celebrating a religious holiday and were all drunk and asleep.

The Gates and Waters

In our spiritual fight with Jezebel and other Babylonian spirits, there are certain Scriptures that seem particularly effective.

> *Thus saith the LORD to his anointed, to Cyrus, whose right hand I have holden, to subdue nations before him; and I will loose the loins of kings, to open before him the two leaved gates; and the gates shall not be shut; I will go before thee, and make the crooked*

places straight: I will break in pieces the gates
of brass, and cut in sunder the bars of iron.
(Isa. 45:1–2)

Another passage important to deliverance is
found in Jeremiah 50:38: "*A drought is upon her*
waters; and they shall be dried up." Jeremiah 51:36
says, "*Therefore thus saith the* LORD; *Behold, I will*
plead thy cause, and take vengeance for thee; and I
will dry up her sea, and make her springs dry."

Both passages not only predicted what has
come to pass for historical Babylon, but also what
God will do to spiritual Babylon in the end times.

Spiritual Babylon

First mention of Babylon in the book of Revelation is found in chapter fourteen, verse eight:
"*And there followed another angel, saying, Babylon*
is fallen, is fallen, that great city, because she made
all nations drink of the wine of the wrath of her for-
nication." This passage portends the fall of that
spiritual city and with it, Satan's kingdom and rule.
All nations drink of her wine and fornicate with her,
yet they have no idea who she is and what she does.

And the great city was divided into three
parts, and the cities of the nations fell: and
great Babylon came in remembrance before
God, to give unto her the cup of the wine of the
fierceness of his wrath.   (Rev. 16:19)

God chose to forget Babylon for a while, but
now He is remembering her and her sins. Her demise is about to take place.

So he carried me away in the spirit into the wilderness: and I saw a woman sit upon a scarlet coloured beast, full of names of blasphemy, having seven heads and ten horns. And the woman was arrayed in purple and scarlet colour, and decked with gold and precious stones and pearls, having a golden cup in her hand full of abominations and filthiness of her fornication: And upon her forehead was a name written, MYSTERY, BABYLON THE GREAT, THE MOTHER OF HARLOTS AND ABOMINATIONS OF THE EARTH. (Rev. 17: 3–5)

The beast is drab, and John's eyes are riveted on the woman. He marvels at her.

Spiritual Babylon rules the earth today. It has great significance to all Christians in the end times. If we are ignorant of her then how can we come out of her, much less counteract and defeat her? Let's see how Babylon the great rules the earth today.

Child Sacrifice

Thousands of infants were killed to please the Babylonian goddess Ashtoreth (also called Astarte, Ashtorah, and Ashtoroth). Next to the temples honoring that hideous goddess were thousands of graves of infants. In *Halley's Bible Handbook* (Halley 1965), it is explained how archaeologists discovered what they believed to be the palace of Jezebel, the chief priestess of the cult of Ashtoreth. In the walls of Jezebel's palace were found jars of infant remains. The jars contained an inscription: "These make me tender and delicate." In their quest to remain tender and delicate (Isa. 47:1), Babylonian women sacrificed their children. Child sacrifice was also rampant in Babylonian worship.

Child sacrifice is being done on an unprecedented scale today. Over one and a half million abortions are performed in America each year, and twenty-six million the world over. Not only that, many children who are not killed are sacrificed on the altars of the world by parents that are so self-centered that they either won't or can't nurture their own children.

Fathers have become separated from their children both physically and mentally. Many have no desire to see their children or take part in their upbringing once they are divorced from the mother. They refuse to pay child support. Worse yet, even if they live with their children, many fathers could not care less about them. The hearts of the fathers have been separated from the hearts of their children.

Today, we have a generation of father-haters because children have abusive, neglectful, or absentee fathers. There is rejection and bitterness everywhere. Girls grow up thinking that they don't need a husband. They have illegitimate children and see no need to marry. A new generation without fathers is emerging in America. Children are being sacrificed on the altars of the world, left to live a life of rejection, depression, hopelessness, and lawlessness. To seek love, they get involved in drugs, sex, or gangs. That's why God said in Malachi:

> *Behold, I will send you Elijah the prophet before the coming of the great and dreadful day*

of the LORD: And he shall turn the heart of the
fathers to the children, and the heart of the
children to their fathers, lest I come and smite
the earth with a curse.   (Malachi 4:5)

The Sexual Revolution

Ancient Babylonian religion worshipped the
flesh. The Babylonians and Egyptians spared nothing for the sake of satisfying their lusts of the flesh.
It was total indulgence in the best of foods, clothing,
shelter, and sex.

Sexual promiscuity, orgies, and rituals were
part of the system. When Moses spent forty days on
the mountain communing with God, the Israelites
gave him up for dead and persuaded Aaron to build
a golden calf. When that was done, they celebrated
by running around naked and having a sexual orgy.

Worship of Baal and Ashtoreth promoted temple prostitution, in which men and women volunteered to serve as prostitutes in order to raise
money for religious activities. Sexual rites included
homosexuality, bestiality, and every disgraceful perversion you can think of. Women and men were
worshipped for their physical beauty. The display of
sexual organs was widespread. The word "groves" in
the Bible refers to places of worship which displayed
huge carvings of both male and female sexual organs.

As spiritual Babylon takes control during the
end times, we will find increasingly widespread sexual promiscuity, fornication, adultery, perversion,
pornography, incest, sexual abuse, bestiality, and
uncleanness.

Greed

> [Babylon traded in] *the merchandise of gold,*
> *and silver, and precious stones, and of pearls,*
> *and fine linen, and purple, and silk, and scar-*
> *let, and all thine wood, and all manner ves-*
> *sels of ivory, and all manner vessels of most*
> *precious wood, and of brass, and iron, and*
> *marble, And cinnamon, and odours, and*
> *ointments, and frankincense, and wine, and*
> *oil, and fine flour, and wheat, and beasts, and*
> *sheep, and horses, and chariots, and slaves,*
> *and souls of men.*　　　　　(Rev. 18:12–13)

All of those items were things of luxury and
avarice. Babylon and Egypt represent greed and
desire for power and luxury.

People plot and kill so that they can obtain fine
things to show that they are worthy to be worshipped. People with an abundance of fine things,
power, and money are greatly admired and emu-
lated. Money and power can provide the best food,
finest clothing, biggest houses and cars, and more
sex. It's pure greed. Greed has become a powerful
ruling spirit in the end times.

Homosexuality and Confusion

Homosexuality is a very powerful, evil spirit
today. It is a total abomination to God and represents
confusion of mind. Confusion is a Babylonian trait.
In Jeremiah 50:2 the Lord says, *"Babylon is taken,*
Bel is confounded." To be confounded is to be confused. Of all the books of the Bible, the book of

Jeremiah uses the word *"confounded"* more than any other. The people of Babylon were confounded or confused, and the same is true today. Later in history, Bel became known as the god Janus, the two-headed god whose symbol is a club which he uses to bash the heads of men. Being two-headed is being double-minded and, therefore, unstable (James 1:8).

Today, homosexuality has reared its ugly head more than at any time in history, except perhaps in the days of decadent Rome. There is no way to compare the two eras because there are no statistics, but homosexuality in America and elsewhere in the world is more blatant and widespread than in the previous thousand years. Despite what the media or homosexual advocacy groups would have us believe, homosexuality is clearly a sin in God's eyes.

> *Do you not know that the wicked will not inherit the kingdom of God? Do not be deceived: Neither the sexually immoral nor idolaters nor adulterers nor male prostitutes nor homosexual offenders.* (1 Cor. 6:9 NIV)

> *Because of this, God gave them over to shameful lusts. Even their women exchanged natural relations for unnatural ones. In the same way the men also abandoned natural relations with women and were inflamed with lust for one another. Men committed indecent acts with other men, and received in themselves the due penalty for their perversion.* (Rom. 1:26–27)

Confusion is increasing today. In the last five years, I have received more cases of schizophrenia, manic depression, and mental/emotional problems than ever before.

Drugs

Widespread use of drugs was a tenet of Babylonian religion. Cocaine was invented in Egypt and probably came from Babylon. Mind-altering drugs were widely used to induce "temple sleep" during which the drugged individuals would hallucinate and see gods, goddesses, heaven, hell, and all kinds of "spiritual" things, including demons.

The poor man's way to hallucinate is through chanting and meditation, albeit slower. Today, drug use is spreading like wildfire. It is western society's latest plague.

Drugs are related to witchcraft. During the Middle Ages, witches used alchemy to produce potions and drugs to control the minds of others. Any time drug use is involved, there is a spirit of Witchcraft. The usual spirit is *Pharmakaea,* the term from the Greek for pharmacy, a place where drugs are prepared and sold.

Astrology, Sorcery, and Witchcraft

Astrology was invented by the Chaldeans, the ruling tribe of Babylon. It was a form of fortune-telling widely used in Babylon and Egypt. Isaiah 47 speaks to the virgin daughter of Babylon:

The loss of children, and widowhood: they

shall come upon thee in their perfection for the multitude of thy sorceries, and for the great abundance of thine enchantments....Stand now with thine enchantments, and with the multitude of thy sorceries, wherein thou has laboured from they youth; if so be thou shalt be able to profit, if so be thou mayest prevail. Thou art wearied in the multitude of thy counsels. Let now the astrologers, the stargazers, the monthly prognosticators, stand up, and save thee from these things that shall come upon thee. (Isa. 47:9, 12–13)

Every major daily newspaper and magazine features horoscopes, and you can watch two or three psychic shows on TV anytime. There has been a great increase in witchcraft and sorcery in the last ten years. Athletes carry good luck charms, presidents consult fortune-tellers, and astrologers become celebrities. It is another sign of Babylon the great.

Murder and Violence

Murder and Violence are characteristic of Babylon. The Babylonians loved violence. Violence reigned in the streets and wars were constant (Jer. 51:46). Today, it is becoming increasingly difficult to walk the streets of most cities at night, and even during the day in some places, with any assurance of safety. Violence and Murder rule the night. TV programs feature violence wholesale—it is impossible for anyone to sit through a night of flipping channels without observing at least 50 acts of violence.

As the end times roll closer, murder and violence will escalate. Satan's beast is going to war against the saints and overcome them. He will kill all of the Christians he can get his hands on. There will be many wars and rumors of war. Kingdoms will war against kingdoms, and there will be much lawlessness (2 Pet. 2:10; Jude 8).

Women's Liberation

The real religious rulers of Babylon were women. The cult of Ashtoreth was so powerful that all women belonged to it. The goddess wife of Baal was even more revered than her male counterpart. Even the men of Israel sat back and allowed their wives to bake cakes to the Queen of Heaven.

The high priestess of the cult of Ashtoreth held a prominent position in the religious and social life of Babylon. She was considered to be a seer and prophetess. The women of Babylon were held in very high esteem. They actually ruled the kingdom.

As the end times approach ever closer, women will take dominant roles in government and business and will control most of the wealth of the world. They will be the leaders in many churches and families. The males will be subjugated and relegated to secondary subservient positions. Women's Liberation will triumph as it never has before.

Come Out of Her, My People

There is little doubt that spiritual Babylon rules the earth today. The fruits are obvious. It is

the devil's mechanism to entrap mankind, especially
Christians, and to bring about the worldwide worship of Satan's beast. All those who are trapped in
that system will taste of the wrath of God. Revelation 18:4 says, *"Come out of her, my people, that ye
be not partakers of her sins, and that ye receive not of
her plagues."* Politically correct agendas supporting
homosexuality, divorce, pornography, drugs, freedom of speech, and abortion will put the nation in
bondage. It's a snare of the fowler that few escape
(Ps. 91:3).

Rulers of Babylon: Beauty and the Beast

Spiritual Babylon is ruled over by a king and a
queen. They are Beauty and the Beast.
Notwithstanding Walt Disney Productions, the
original story of beauty and the beast is found in
Revelation chapter seventeen. The apostle John saw
a woman sitting on a beast.

> *And the woman was arrayed in purple and
> scarlet colour, and decked with gold and pre-
> cious stones and pearls, having a golden cup
> in her hand full of abominations and filthi-
> ness of her fornication.* (Rev. 17:4)

The woman is the headliner, the one on top, the
name on the marquee. She is beautiful and alluring.
She is the titular head of Babylon. *"And upon her
forehead was a name written, MYSTERY, BABYLON
THE GREAT, THE MOTHER OF HARLOTS AND
ABOMINATIONS OF THE EARTH"* (Rev. 17:5). She's a
mystery because *"none seeth"* her (Isa. 47:10).

Babylon the great is a worldwide spiritual power. All nations fornicate with her. The angel told John, *"The waters which thou sawest, where the whore sitteth, are peoples, and multitudes, and nations, and tongues"* (Rev. 17:15). She has many admirers and worshippers—maybe even you.

She is Jezebel, and yet she is much more. Her rulership extends throughout the world into the body of Christ, families, politics, professions, businesses, relationships, and most things.

The beast is the guy behind the scenes, the prop. For the time being, he chooses to lay back in the shadows like the hunchback of Notre Dame. But don't pity him. He represents the spirit of Ahab. He is the other ruler of spiritual Babylon.

Jezebel and Ahab—The Royal Line

We are interested in the historical Jezebel and Ahab because a person with the Jezebel spirit will exhibit the characteristics of the historical Jezebel, and a person with the Ahab spirit will manifest the nature of the historical Ahab. Jezebel and Ahab are of importance to us because they were worshippers of Babylonian gods and goddesses, so a study of their lives gives us insight as to how these spirits operate.

To understand Jezebel and Ahab, we need to go to first Kings chapter sixteen. Omri was the father of Ahab who ruled Israel before Ahab. He was the most evil king up to his day. First Kings 16:25 says, *"But Omri wrought evil in the eyes of the LORD, and did worse than all that were before him."* Ahab, however, was more than a chip off the old block. He outdid his father. Verse thirty says, *"And Ahab the son of Omri did evil in the sight of the Lord above all that were before him."* Ahab was the champion evil king. Why?

For one thing, the kings of Israel were supposed to marry Jewish women, but Ahab married Jezebel, the daughter of the king of Zidon who worshipped Baal. You see, Jezebel was a beautiful woman and Ahab was a man of sexual lust. He was also self-centered. He knew what he wanted and no one was going to deny him, even God. Ahab took God lightly. Ahab not only married Jezebel, he worshipped her gods and served Baal (v. 31). He built temples and altars to Baal, and built groves (v. 33). Ahab was a pushover for a pretty face.

Ahab men are like that. Sex and good looks mean more to them than God. They will reason away the commandments of God in order to justify indulging in their worldly pursuits. "God doesn't mind us having sex; after all, sex is a gift from God. Look at David, he had hundreds of wives and concubines." Ahab men love sex and often delve into pornography, fornication, adultery, masturbation, and eventually different forms of perversion, depending on each individual's taste and degree of control. Their desires for the things of the world far outweigh their concern for their own children.

Ahab even permitted child sacrifice in Israel.

In Ahab's time, Hiel of Bethel rebuilt Jericho. He laid its foundations at the cost of his first-born son Abiram, and he set up its gates at the

> *cost of his youngest son Segub, in accordance*
> *with the word of the LORD spoken by Joshua*
> *son of Nun.*   (1 Kings 16:25)

If his wife wants an abortion, Ahab will say, "It's up to you," and then help with the arrangements.

Ahab was the king of Israel, but he refused responsibility. Ahab men are mostly irresponsible. They are spoiled, lazy, and slothful idolaters.

Jezebel was the head priestess of the cult of Ashtoreth. She not only worshipped Ashtoreth, she determined to annihilate all of God's prophets. In 1 Kings chapter eighteen, we find that Jezebel and Ahab were looking for Elijah to kill him. They had already wiped out many of God's prophets and leaders.

Babylon the great (Jezebel) has wiped out the prophets of God for centuries, even after Jesus ascended to heaven.

> *And I saw the woman drunken with the blood*
> *of the saints, and with the blood of the martyrs*
> *of Jesus: and when I saw her, I wondered with*
> *great admiration.*   (Rev. 17:6)

Revelation 18:24 says, "*And in her was found the blood of prophets, and of saints, and of all that were slain upon the earth.*" She's a murdering spirit with Death as her servant. She is trying to kill you, and she is trying to kill me.

In 1 Kings chapter twenty-one, Ahab coveted Naboth's vineyard. Ahab had many vineyards and Naboth had only a tiny one. Ahab went to Naboth and asked to buy or trade for Naboth's vineyard.

Naboth replied, *"The LORD forbid it me, that I should give the inheritance of my fathers unto thee"* (v. 3). Naboth was a good man, and he knew he was not to give away an inheritance from God. But Ahab was greedy. Ahab went back to his palace upset, shut himself in his bedroom, laid himself on his bed, faced the wall, and refused to eat.

Ahab men are cry-babies and pouters when they cannot get what they want, and are weak and lazy. However, Jezebel was smarter and more aggressive. When she inquired what was the matter, Ahab lied to her by failing to mention that Naboth's vineyard was an inheritance and could not be given to anyone outside the family (v. 6). Ahab men are liars.

Jezebel said, *"Dost thou now govern the kingdom of Israel? arise, and eat bread, and let thine heart be merry: I will give thee the vineyard of Naboth the Jezreelite"* (1 Kings 21:7). In other words, she put her husband down. "What kind of a king are you? Alright, don't worry, I'll get you the vineyard." Ahab had no guts, so he let his wife do it. Jezebel wrote letters in Ahab's name, sealed them with his seal, and sent them to various people with instructions to set Naboth up through false witnessing. Naboth was stoned to death.

When Jezebel announced that Naboth was dead, Ahab gleefully went to claim Naboth's vineyard. Ahab men are users of women. They allow the women to lead and take responsibility because the women will get them what they want. Behind every Jezebel woman is an Ahab man, whether it is her husband, boyfriend, or father.

Some women will say to their husbands, "What kind of man are you? I'll do it." Husbands give up and say, "Go ahead, you do it!" Ahab willingly abdicated his throne to Jezebel. Jezebel women try to take illegal command wherever they work, live, or worship. They are the heads of the families, the high priest of the homes, and try to gain control in their local churches. They have a murderous spirit and will kill their husbands and children spiritually if not physically. Jezebel women will bear false witness when it is profitable, especially against church leaders in order to discredit them.

Ahab men are double-minded compromisers. In first Kings chapter twenty, the powerful Syrian army twice came against Israel. Both times a prophet of God came to Ahab and told him that God was going to give a mighty miracle to Ahab and defeat the Syrians. God indeed routed the Syrians twice. Still, Ahab did not return to worshipping God. Yet, he inquired of God's prophets when he wanted help (1 Kings 22:6). He went back and forth—truly a double-minded man. Ahab men go to church if it is politically correct or for personal gain, not because they love God. They witness God's miracles and still refuse to come to the Lord.

Jezebel is a witch by definition and action. Witchcraft is manipulation and control of others through demonic means. She seeks to control the minds of others through lies, complaining, threats, position, shame, pity, and whatever else she can use.

Manifestations in the Family

A Jezebel wife manipulates and controls the family. She may use sexual deprivation or excessive desire to control her husband. Ahab is a rejected, insecure individual, subject to withdrawal and low self-esteem, so he will beg for sex if necessary. On the other hand, she will use excessive lust and desire for sex. If Ahab is not able to keep up, he turns into an inferior male who cannot satisfy his wife. For fear of losing her, he will do many things and let her have control.

Jezebel will have her way. She can be sweet, boisterous, or a clinging vine. She uses charm, smiles, soothing touches, threats, temper tantrums, anger, or anything else that's necessary. Doing the work and taking responsibility are part of the price for being a Jezebel. She doesn't trust Ahab to do anything anyway.

If she is physically attractive, she often seduces men. She feels more comfortable with men if she knows that they are attracted to her because then she has a measure of control over them. She will cheat on her husband; she's a harlot, after all. Her husband, on the other hand, is just as bad. Since he loves sex, he will be a cad—if he has enough courage.

Ahab avoids confrontation and lets his wife have her own way. He has given up on being the leader. He's the one watching TV all day while his wife is busy running around and working. He is more interested in gratifying his own desires without too much energy being spent in the process.

Ahab men may believe there is a God, but it's not worth it to commit their lives to Him. Their lusts for the flesh and world are too great to give up. Jezebel receives the head position because Ahab doesn't want it. Ahab's main characteristics are carelessness and irresponsibility. He simply can't be bothered. So long as he has his porno collection (out of sight of the kids, of course), he is content. As long as he can have his pleasures and pursuits of the world, she can do anything she wants.

Ahab abdicates his head position as priest of the family. Jezebel is the one that carts the kids to church every Sunday and attends meetings during the week. He doesn't care. He hides in the bedroom when the church gang is at the house. He has a million excuses, from blaming the hypocrites in the church to his need for rest. Ahab may even encourage his wife to go to church. It gets her out of his hair and gives him more time for his own delights.

If Ahab is persuaded to show up in church, he does it begrudgingly or with minimal effort. He's hardly enthusiastic about church projects. He hangs back, or, if forced to engage in church affairs, he runs from leadership. Emptying the garbage can is about the only responsibility he wants. Jezebel is the more spiritual one, he is just her supporter.

It's not that Ahab is physically weak. He can be strong and athletic. After all, Ahab was a warrior too. He loved battle; it was like a game to him. Ahabs love sports. If they cannot participate, they love to watch on TV or go to the games and fights. It gives them vicarious identities.

Female Problems

A sign of Jezebel is problems with the female reproductive tract. Women with the Jezebel spirit often have severe menstrual cramps and bleeding. They are frequently barren or have miscarriages, still-born infants, and abortions. Jezebel resides in their sexual organs. She hates women. Eventually, the Jezebel woman may have a hysterectomy, breast cancer, or something similar.

Mind you, throughout all of this, both the Ahab man and the Jezebel woman will not see what is happening. It is a spiritual attack.

The Children

Children in a Babylonian family take on the same characteristics as those of their parents, only sometimes worse. Girls become man-haters, aggressive, and disrespectful. Daughters tend to be interested in witchcraft as a means of gaining control over people and obtaining power. Boys become soft, self-centered, lazy, and mamma's boys. They use women. They feel rejected and, therefore, become cry-babies. Both are spiritually dead.

Both genders are apt to be involved in sexual promiscuity, drugs, or crime. Homosexuality and lesbianism are more serious results of a curse of Jezebel on the family.

Divorces in the family are prevalent signs of Jezebel. In one family I know of, all three sons were divorced and living with their mother—mamma's boys for sure. Both daughters were also divorced

and living with men. Daughters-in-law find it difficult to get along with their mothers-in-law. After all,
there can be only one queen in the family. When
Ahab and Jezebel are in the family, it is a little
Babylon.

In the Church

The church must deal with Jezebel, or she will
kill it with spiritual death. I suspect that many of
the problems pastors have in leading the sheep are
due to the Jezebel spirit. She will cause church
splits, dryness, and slumber.

God specifically warns about her:

> *Notwithstanding I have a few things against
> thee, because thou sufferest that woman Jeze-
> bel, which calleth herself a prophetess, to
> teach and to seduce my servants to commit
> fornication, and to eat things sacrificed unto
> idols. And I gave her space to repent of her
> fornication; and she repented not. Behold, I
> will cast her into a bed, and them that commit
> adultery with her into great tribulation, except
> they repent of their deeds. And I will kill her
> children with death; and all the churches
> shall know that I am he which searcheth the
> reins and hearts: and I will give unto every
> one of you according to your works.* (Rev. 2:20)

Jezebel loves to prophesy because it is a way of
controlling people. "Thus sayeth the Lord" is a powerful tool used to manipulate the saints and the
leaders. After all, who dares to disobey God? She

loves to teach and seduce the saints for several reasons. First, she wants to be head priestess in the church. She sometimes has her own group of intercessors or Bible class at her home. She draws the sheep to her, and they begin to adore and pay attention to her words. Then, she subtly makes negative remarks about those in leadership to erode their power. She often prophesies in church. If she can get close to the prophet or pastor of the church, she will then be able to make suggestions to the leaders on what the church should do. She will destroy the vision of the church and its efforts to stay on the narrow path. "God showed me this" and "God told me that" are frequently used expressions by a Jezebel.

Death

A Jezebel woman can sit in the pew, look at a speaker, and send worms of death against that person. The woman herself doesn't have the slightest idea that Jezebel is using her eyes to curse another.

If the pastor sympathizes with her, he will lose. Pastors who suffer from rejection will have a difficult time with her. His desires to please and compromise give her more room. Because she is often the most religious and zealous person in church, she will have a following, so he will back off instead of lose sheep. Jezebel, of course, knows this instinctively.

Don't get me wrong. There are many wonderful woman called by God to be leaders in the church. But there is a difference. Those leaders are humble, submissive, and unpretentious. Of course, the same rules apply to male leaders. Male leaders who are proud and unsubmissive to no one are just male Jezebels. Cults are full of them, and the body of Christ suffers from both kinds.

Again, the culprit behind Jezebel is Ahab. The church is full of weak-willed wishy-washy male leaders who compromise the word of God and allow people in the church to go on sinning. They worry that if they come down hard, the saints will go to another church. The more money a saint donates to the church, the more leeway he receives.

The Fruits Do Not Lie

It is often difficult to detect the working of Jezebel and Ahab spirits in a family or person. Both can be loving, zealous, and kind people. You must go by their fruits. A corrupt tree cannot give good fruit, and a good tree cannot give corrupt fruit. Look at the family situation and what is happening in church. Look for the fruits of Jezebel and Ahab. You cannot deny the fruits (Matt. 7:17–18).

Do not misunderstand; if a person has the flu, don't condemn the person, condemn the flu. If a person has cancer, sympathize with the person and pray for his or her recovery. If a person has a Jezebel or Ahab spirit, love him or her and pray for his release. Don't accuse him—deliver him.

The All-Time Great Deception

While looking at Jezebel, we tend to forget Ahab. They are like beauty and the beast. Ahab pushes the woman into the limelight. Jezebel is not the main character to get rid of, nor is she the more evil of the two. Ahab is usually a delightful and easy person to get along with because he is laid-back, but in actuality Ahab is the culprit. God looks at the hearts and reins of men because the evil that started the whole mess is found deep within. God knows that it is the Ahab spirit that opens the door for Jezebel to come in and take over.

I want to make this very clear. It is the Ahab spirit that is most evil. The Bible says that Ahab was the most evil king of Israel that ever lived (1 Kings 21:25). The Bible never compares queens. God judged Ahab first, and Ahab died long before Jezebel. God gives men authority and therefore holds them accountable for their families. Accordingly, the men will be held responsible if the spirit of Jezebel is in their families. Likewise, God will first judge pastors if they allow Jezebel women to run the churches.

Women, You're Being Used

King Ahab used Queen Jezebel. If it were not profitable, Ahab spirits would not allow Jezebel spirits to take over. Men will allow women to lead if there is something in it for them. When the time is right, Ahab brushes Jezebel aside in order to take over. Women's lib is a deception. Instead of women taking authority, men should be forced to take their God-given responsibility.

Remember how in Revelation 17, Babylon the great is richly adorned and celebrated? She sits on a beast, and the spotlight is upon her. But look at verse 16: "*And the ten horns which thou sawest upon the beast, these shall hate the whore, and shall make her desolate and naked, and shall eat her flesh, and burn her with fire.*" You know why? Because it is time for the beast to take over. He utterly deserts her, hates her, and dumps her. Not only that, but he makes her desolate and naked, eats her flesh, and burns her with fire. After all, she is only a deceived fool. Ha! She thinks that she is the leader, but in the very end Ahab grabs back the throne.

> *And it was given unto him* [the beast] *to make war with the saints, and to overcome them: and power was given him over all kindreds, and tongues, and nations. And all that dwell upon the earth shall worship him, whose names are not written in the book of life of the Lamb slain from the foundation of the world.*
>
> (Rev. 13:7–8)

My, my. Where is the woman? I thought the beast loves the woman and wants her on top. Isn't it funny how he destroys her so that he can take over the world and have all of mankind worship him alone as god?

Why is it that in Revelation 19:19, it is the beast that challenges Jesus in the final battle of the ages? Where is the woman? Don't you see that it is all a sham and deception? Women are being used today by the men of the world who are Ahabs. The men have no intention of sharing the throne with women in the spirit of equality. It is to their advantage to let women think that they are equal.

Now, women have to work harder than ever and take equal (no, more) responsibility for the family. Women think their sexual freedoms are a step in the right direction, yet lustful men never had it so good. Men now indulge much more freely. That's why they don't care for their children. Why should they? There's so much more fun outside of their families. Anyway, it's the woman's responsibility now, not theirs. Instead of forcing men to take responsibility, women gleefully allow themselves to be deceived and used. Ahab is a dastardly spirit— hateful and conniving, even more so than Jezebel. He is the gatekeeper, the door opener, the one who says, "Go ahead, be my guest." He will be judged severely.

Adam and Eve: The First Ahab and Jezebel

It all started with Adam and Eve in the Garden of Eden. Some Christians contend that Adam took the fruit from Eve and ate it because of his great love for her; he couldn't refuse her because of his love. That's very romantic, but a big piece of baloney. First Timothy 2:14 says, "*And Adam was not deceived, but the woman being deceived was in the transgression.*"

If Adam was not deceived, what was he? He was standing in the background listening as the serpent deceived Eve. He was not fooled, so he had the responsibility to stop the serpent and prevent Eve from eating the fruit of the Tree of Knowledge of Good and Evil. After all, with his prodigious mind, he knew that God had said that they would die if they ate the fruit. Adam ate the fruit with full understanding. Why? Because Adam had already deceived himself. He had already formed the idea that if he ate the forbidden fruit, he would be a god.

However, Adam didn't have the guts to do it himself, so he used Eve. When Adam allowed Eve to be deceived and eat the fruit, he was using her as a scapegoat and guinea pig. If they got away with it, good. If not, he could blame her. When God caught Adam, he said *"The woman whom thou gavest to be with me, she gave me of the tree, and I did eat"* (Gen. 3:12).

Adam passed the buck. He refused to take responsibility for his actions. He played the victim, and blamed Eve. In effect, Adam said to God, "Don't kill me, kill her." Does that sound like love?

When God threatened to kill all of Israel for her idolatry and disobedience, Moses stepped in and said, *"Yet now, if thou wilt forgive their sin—; and if not, blot me, I pray thee, out of thy book which thou hast written"* (Exod. 32:32). Moses was innocent, yet Moses said, "Kill me, I'll take the responsibility." Jesus Christ, the Last Adam (1 Cor. 15:45), said, *"Father, forgive them; for they know not what they do"* (Luke 23:34). Though completely innocent of sin and transgression, out of love He assumed the responsibility.

There was no love in Adam and no submission in Eve. Eve never bothered to ask Adam his opinion or permission (although it probably would not have done any good); therefore, she overstepped the authority God had given Adam. That is called rebellion.

So Paul said in Ephesians 5:22, "*Wives, submit yourselves unto your own husband, as unto the Lord.*" And he said in verse 25, "*Husbands, love your wives, even as Christ also loved the church, and gave himself for it.*" Paul was simply trying to establish the kingdom of God in the family. The very character of Jesus is love and submission to the Father, while the very character of Satan is hatred and rebellion. You cannot separate love from submission. It is impossible to truly love without humility which leads to submission, and you cannot truly have a submissive heart without love. They are the two sides of the same coin: God's coin is love and submission; Satan's coin is hate and rebellion. One is fueled by humility, the other by pride.

Restored to the Garden of Eden

God wants to lead us back to the Garden of Eden and restore everything that Adam lost. But we cannot get there with the heart of the First Adam; only with the nature of the Last Adam, Jesus Christ, can we return. Ahab and Jezebel are the character of the fallen Adam and Eve; two sides of the same coin, they cleave as one. Both hate and pride come from the very pit of hell. Remember, "*The beast that thou sawest was, and is not; and shall ascend out of the bottomless pit*" (Rev. 17:8). He brought the woman with him, but he's worse than the woman. He brings her with him as a scapegoat, a facade, a double deception to deceive both the woman and the world. He hates the woman. So does Satan.

Satan Hates Women

Everywhere that I give mass deliverance, I find that for every man that falls on the ground, there are five to ten more women. Why are more women attacked and demonized? The answer is found in Genesis 3:15. When God passed judgment, He first cursed the serpent (v. 14). Then He cursed the woman with these words: *"And I will put enmity between thee and the woman, and between thy seed and her seed; it shall bruise thy head, and thou shalt bruise his heel."*

God put enmity between the serpent and the woman. Satan has a special hatred for women and will attack them first and most severely. Women are Satan's designated enemies. It was Adam's failure to love and protect Eve that led to this curse. to protect the women against Satan, we men are called to love and provide spiritual protection or coverage for them. Failure to do so will leave our women exposed to the devil, and men will be judged.

In many ways women are usually more spiritual than men. Women know how to suffer, sacrifice, and have a greater capacity to love than most men, but they are more easily deceived and tricked because of that. That's why we men need to take greater steps to protect our women from demonic attack. God said, *"thy desire shall be to thy husband, and he shall rule over thee"* (v. 16). God wasn't putting women down. On the contrary, He was giving them protection against Satan.

Come on, husband, do your job. Don't let Satan eat up your wife and family. It's your responsibility.

Tame your desire for fleshy pursuits, and be the head priest God called you to be. It doesn't mean that you have to manipulate, dominate, or lord it over your wife. That's not love: it's being a male Jezebel. God didn't call your wife to quit being a Jezebel so that you can be one.

Isaiah 47

I am taking ample time to discuss Babylon the great and the spirits of Ahab and Jezebel because spiritual warfare will inevitably and eventually lead to those powerful spirits and to Satan's evil system. We need to know our enemy, what our weapons are, and how to use them against the enemy. Isaiah chapter forty-seven exposes both the system and the spirits in Babylon.

> *Come down, and sit in the dust, O virgin daughter of Babylon, sit on the ground: there is no throne, O daughter of the Chaldeans: for thou shalt no more be called tender and delicate.* (Isa. 47:1)

There is no doubt that this chapter is talking about Babylon the great. She calls herself the virgin daughter of Babylon.

Isaiah 47:9 says, "*these two things shall come to thee in a moment in one day, the loss of children, and widowhood.*"

It is interesting that this spirit says,

> *I sit a queen, and am no widow, and shall see no sorrow. Therefore shall her plagues come in one day, death, and mourning, and famine;*

and she shall be utterly burned with fire: for
strong is the Lord God who judgeth her.

(Rev. 18:7–8)

Therefore, the virgin daughter of Babylon in Isaiah 47:1 is the same spirit found in Revelation 17 and 18.

This spirit considers herself a queen, the ruler of all the earth. She sits on a throne and calls herself the virgin. She is a whore but disguises herself as pure, chaste, and desirable. She is an impostor. There is no throne for her. She wants to be tender and delicate, but she is an old hag. She has killed many infants to keep her tender and delicate.

Some cosmetic firms collect placentas and fetuses to dry them up, grind them into powder, and put them into facial creams. Women use them on the walls of their palaces—the skin of their faces, to keep them tender and delicate.

As the goddess of Babylon she is the virgin mother of the sun god named Tammuz. She is called the lady of kingdoms (Isa. 47:5), and queen of heaven (Jeremiah 44:17–19, 25). She claims to be equal to God. In fact, she says, *"I am, and none else beside me"* (Isa. 47:8). Some think that she is an evil spirit masquerading as the Virgin Mary of the Roman Catholic church. She loves to be worshipped. She has had many other names through history, such as Mother of all knowledge, the Mediatrix, Mother of all mankind, and Mother of all apostles and saints. She is called Aphrodite, Venus, Kali, Pele, Cybele, Astarte, Ashtoreth, and countless other names. Perhaps Jane, Louise, and Jennifer, who knows?

She has no mercy on the old (Isa. 47:6). She kills them with disease and death. I've looked at women on their death beds, and Jezebel has stared back at me through their eyes. She can kill you too.

Jezebel loves sorcery, witchcraft, and astrology. She is the author of such things because she loves to manipulate and to control the lives of others. (See Isaiah 47:9, 12–13). If you find occultic activity, she is there.

Schizophrenia, Rejection, and Rebellion

We're rounding third base and coming home. Let's expose Satan's end-time scheme.

In order to fully understand what Satan's scheme is, we need to refer to a fine book on deliverance—Frank and Ida Mae Hammond's *Pigs in the Parlor*. In the chapter entitled "Schizophrenia," Ida Mae explains that they had been ministering deliverance to a woman for months with no permanent results. One morning after praying over the problem, God spoke to Ida Mae and explained that the woman had schizophrenia. God had Ida Mae put her two hands on the table, palms downward. Then He had her trace her hands on a sheet of paper. God had Ida Mae put down the names of demons on each finger and on the flat of her hands. A copy of that diagram is provided in Appendix A at the end of this book.

These spirits represent the nest of spirits that make up schizophrenia or double-mindedness. "*A double-minded man is unstable in all his ways*" (James 1:8). The left hand represents the hand of rejection; the right hand is the hand of rebellion. God had Ida Mae put her hands together, with fingers interlocking. As she separated her two hands, the thumbs were the first to come apart; next came the pinkie fingers, then the forefingers, then the ring fingers, and finally, the middle fingers.

To set people free from schizophrenia (God's definition, not psychiatry's), deal with the demons on the thumbs first, then the pinkie fingers, and so on. Then address those on the flat of the hands. However, when it comes to the right hand, you need to deal with the root of bitterness from the beginning.[1]

Clinical schizophrenia results when the nest is full-blown. Even though people may have some of the spirits in the nest, that does not make them schizophrenics. But if they yield to more and more of those spirits, their conditions worsen and they start to exhibit more of the full-blown traits. A mature schizophrenic is out of control, given to hearing voices and subject to sweeping mood swings with emotional outbursts. His mind is confused and he is unable to function normally. His testimony has been completely annihilated.

It is Satan's way to imprison and control minds. As he controls minds, they begin to look more and more like the people described in 2 Peter 2:3–19. These individuals will be given to sexual lust, filthy conversation, lawlessness, walking after the flesh,

---

[1] Frank and Ida Mae Hammond, *Pigs in the Parlor* (Impact Christian Books, Inc., 332 Leffingwell #101, Kirkwood, MO 63122, ©1973), pp. 123–129.

despising government and leaders, self-will, speaking evil of dignities, corruption, adultery, covetousness, cursed children, greed, living in darkness, and wantonness. In verses seven through thirteen, Jude describes schizophrenics in much the same language.

That's Satan end-time plan for mankind. Why do I say that? Because the two hands of schizophrenia describes with great accuracy the characteristics of Ahab and Jezebel.

Ahab—The Left Hand of Rejection

The left hand of rejection is the hand of Ahab. Ahab is full of fears, sexual lust, insecurity, self pity, fantasy, depression, jealousy, envy, hopelessness, guilt, shame, and pouting.

Jezebel—The Right Hand of Rebellion

"For rebellion is as the sin of witchcraft, and stubbornness is as iniquity and idolatry" (1 Sam. 15:23). The right hand shows demons of Stubbornness, Self-Will, Selfishness, Confrontation, Control, Possessiveness, Hatred, Resentment, Murder, and Bitterness—certainly an accurate description of Jezebel.

Remember, you cannot separate Ahab and Jezebel. They are two sides of the same coin, two hands with fingers intertwined. To successfully wage war against Ahab and Jezebel, you need to know the spirits involved in schizophrenia.

Schizophrenia always starts off with rejection. Since all of us have suffered rejection in one form or other, rejection may be the starter, but the catalyst is unforgiveness and bitterness. If a person is rejected he or she often holds bitterness and hatred. If the bitterness continues, it breaks out into open rebellion.

A person with the Ahab spirit will also have the Jezebel spirit and vice versa. It's only a question of which is dominant. In a man, Ahab is usually dominant, but not always. There are male Jezebels. Women usually turn to outward and external rebellion. The male rebels are more sneaky and quiet. Nevertheless, he is rebellious from head to toe. One is inward, the other outward.

A Jezebel woman has invariably suffered deep rejection and hurt, particularly from her father. If she harbors resentment, unforgiveness, and bitterness, it turns into a hate or love/hate relationship with her father or other men. Forgiveness is the key to setting her free. She has to forgive and let go. Sometimes, inner healing, especially of memories, is necessary to complete the deliverance. Taking out the demons without healing may leave her with scars and hurts that open the door for future demonic attack.

Jezebel women avoid fear and rejection by trying to control every situation, even if it means using manipulation and witchcraft. They find a need to lead and maintain dominance. A loving and protective husband takes away the need for that.

An Ahab man needs to handle the rejection in his life along with the accompanying fears. He usually has several different fears. As with the Jezebel spirit, he needs to handle unforgiveness, resentment, and rebellion.

Men are usually not as open as women to deliverance or counseling. They still want to protect their egos. Rejected people build icy walls around their hearts in order to avoid future hurt. They have few friends. If they are threatened, they withdraw behind their walls, which are sometimes so thick they cannot receive the love of God. Ask God to melt them. Usually, rejected people are starved for love because so little filters through the walls. If you love them today, they are happy; but tomorrow is another day, and today's love is not good enough. They look at the world through glasses of rejection and fear.

Casting Out the Jezebel Spirit

The Jezebel person must reverse everything that gave that spirit the right to enter. Forgiveness is a must. Spend a lot of time leading the person through forgiveness. Since unforgiveness brings heavy curses, one should also break the curse of unforgiveness.

The women (since it is usually found in women) must become humble and submissive in order to create an atmosphere in direct opposition to Jezebel's pride and lack of submission. The spirit hates it and is weakened by it. Women must also avoid going back to old attitudes, for the wrong attitudes give strength to the spirit.

Renounce all forms of witchcraft, strange religions, fortune-telling, and occultic activities. If there is a known activity, renounce it specifically. Announce to Satan that they will not follow him or his ways because they belong to the Lord Jesus.

Bind up the ruling spirits of Rejection and Rebellion in the heavenlies. Cut all of the soul ties with husbands, other males, and even female figures who have had negative effects on their lives.

Also, cut any soul ties with mothers and other female family members who may have the same spirit. This spirit frequently comes down the family line.

When praying against this spirit, dry up her waters and knock her gates and walls down, all while claiming the blood of Jesus. Jezebel's strategy will be to throw up lesser spirits to block the way. You may need to cast out an array of lesser spirits such as Anger, Resentment, Suicide, and Unforgiveness. Cast them out and continue to pursue her. She will run into the inner chambers of that person, usually in the marrow of the spine or into the female organs. The Holy Spirit will tell you where she is hiding.

Cut her off from all other spirits in the room or the heavenlies. If the Jezebel spirit is in other people in the room, the spirit can draw strength from other people.

When she starts to scream, she is probably trapped and reaching the end of her rope. She is weakening and scared. (I talk about it as a "she," but actually the spirit has no gender.) She usually comes out with wailing. It is generally a prolonged, high-pitched scream. This same scream is often evident when casting out Witchcraft. Continue to put the pressure on.

Sometimes the workers see her as a fat, naked woman having her hair combed by many attendants.

She is also seen as a black spider with a beautiful face wearing bright red lipstick.

Casting Out the Ahab Spirit

Deliverance from the Ahab spirit is almost identical to deliverance from the Jezebel spirit, except that there is more fear and rejection involved. Insecurities are more prominent, and the person usually requires continued counseling to teach him how to become responsible and change his habits.

The afflicted person must make the decision to change his ways. An Ahab man often has many bad habits: masturbation, drugs, alcohol, and gambling. To break them, he needs to continue walking with the Lord and reaffirming his desire to change.

He is often seen as a little boy crying behind thick walls. There is a great degree of Witchcraft Mind Control over him, which may be pictured as dark bands around his head and body. These bands look like metal straps around a wooden barrel. Melt the walls of rejection, and loose the chains around his mind.

Ask God to send His angels to recover the fragments of the tormented mind that have been stolen through witchcraft, to bring them back, to put them in proper order, and to quicken them to the individual.

To defeat Ahab, the deliveree must decide to be responsible for his wife and family, moving from reticence and passivity into following God's example of responsibility. God is the most responsible person in the universe. He took the responsibility of restoring and bringing us back to the Garden of Eden. That's why Jesus died for us.

In Summary

There are other aspects of Satan's kingdom and end-time scheme to capture the minds of men and women, but the above gives you some idea and plan of attack to free the people of God. I've attempted to show you the entire forest so that you don't get stuck looking at one tree. Knowing the enemy's overall scheme gives you the ability to know how Satan is moving through a family or church. Remember also to protect the women and never embarrass them by calling them a Jezebel.

Chapter Four

Satan's Rights

Satan cannot torment without a right established by God. He knows every "legal" right God gives him and will absolutely refuse to leave if those rights remain. In order to cast out demons you need to destroy Satan's legal rights over that person, place, or group. Even when sheer strength of the Word of God and persistency forces demons out, if legal rights remain, then demons promptly enter again.

Legal rights are sometimes called "curses." Garbage attracts flies and rats. Flies are like ruling spirits in the heavenlies and rats are like rulers of darkness on earth. Get rid of the garbage, and the flies and rats disappear. On the other hand, if the garbage remains, they invariably come back. Therefore, the problem is not so much getting rid of demons as it is eliminating garbage.

Curses of Iniquity

And the LORD passed by before him, and proclaimed, The LORD, The LORD God, merciful and gracious, longsuffering, and abundant in

*goodness and truth, Keeping mercy for thou-
sands, forgiving iniquity and transgression
and sin, and that will by no means clear the
guilty; visiting the iniquity of the fathers upon
the children, and upon the children's children, unto the third and to the fourth generation.* (Exod. 34:6–7)

The same is found in Exodus 20:5 and repeated in
Deuteronomy 5:9 and Numbers 14:18.

Very few families possess "clean" ancestries,
untainted by any occultic involvement or idolatry.
One sin in particular, illegitimacy, brings curses
down even unto the tenth generation (Deut. 23:2).
Many saints suffer torment, misfortune, accidents,
and poverty without knowing why. This includes
practicing Christians who love God, tithe on a
regular basis, read their Bibles daily, and attend
church three times a week. Yet they unknowingly
live under a curse sent down the generations. Many
are tormented by occultic spirits because their ancestors practiced witchcraft, fortune-telling, or other
occultic activity.

Listed below are fifty-nine curses, thanks to
Win Worley's excellent books on deliverance, *The
Hosts of Hell* series. Another excellent book is Derek
Prince's book *Blessing or Curse*.

Biblical Curses

Sins bring curses. *"The curse causeless shall
not come"* (Prov. 26:2). We are discussing curses
which have been pronounced by God not hexes that
come from witches and other people.

1. Those who curse or mistreat Jews (Gen. 12:3; Num. 24:9)
2. Against willing deceivers (Josh. 9:22–23; Jer. 48:10; Mal. 1:14; Gen. 27:12)
3. On adulterous women (Num. 5:27)
4. Disobedience to the Lord's commandments (Deut. 11:28; Dan. 9:11; Jer. 11:3)
5. Idolatry (Jer. 44:8; Deut. 29:18–20; Exod. 20:5; Deut. 5:8–9)
6. Those who keep or own cursed objects (Deut. 7:25; Josh. 6:18)
7. Refusing to come to the Lord's help (Judg. 5:23)
8. House of the wicked (Prov. 3:33)
9. Refusing to give to the poor (Prov. 28:27)
10. The earth, because of man's disobedience (Isa. 24:3–6)
11. Jerusalem is a curse to all nations if Jews rebel against God (Jer. 26:4–6)
12. Thieves and those who swear falsely by the Lord's name (Zech. 5:4)
13. Ministers who fail to give the glory to God (Mal. 2:1–2)
14. Those who rob God of tithes and offerings (Mal. 3:8–9)
15. Those who hearken unto their wives rather than God (Gen. 3:17)
16. Those who dishonor their parents (Deut. 27:16)
17. Those who create graven images (Deut. 27:15)
18. Those who willfully cheat people out of their properties (Deut. 27:17)
19. Those who take advantage of blind people. (Deut 27:18)
20. Those who oppress strangers, widows, or fatherless (Deut. 27:19; Exod. 22:22–24)
21. He who lies with his father's wife (Deut. 27:20)

22. He who lies with any beast (Deut. 27:21; Exod. 22:19)
23. He who lies with his sister (incest) (Deut. 27:22)
24. Those who smite their neighbors secretly (Deut. 27:24)
25. Those who take money to slay the innocent (Deut. 27:25)
26. Adulterers (Deut. 22:22–27; Job 24:15–18).
27. The proud (Ps. 119:21)
28. Those who trust in man and not the Lord (Jer. 17:5)
29. Those who do the work of the Lord deceitfully (Jer. 48:10)
30. Those who keep back the sword from blood (Jer. 48:10; 1 Kings 20:35–42)
31. Those who reward evil for good (Prov. 17:13)
32. Illegitimate children (for 10 generations) (Deut. 23:2)
33. Murderers (Exod. 21:12)
34. Those who murder deliberately(Exod. 21:14)
35. Children who strike their parents (Exod. 21:15)
36. Kidnappers (Exod. 21:16; Deut. 24:7)
37. Those who curse their parents (Exod. 21:17)
38. Those who cause the unborn to die (Exod. 21:22–23)
39. Those who do not prevent death (Exod. 21:29)
40. Witchcraft practitioners (Exod. 22:18)
41. Those who sacrifice to fake gods (Exod. 22:20)
42. Those who attempt to turn anyone away from the Lord (Deut. 13:6–18)
43. Those who follow horoscopes (astrology) (Deut. 17:2–5)
44. Those who rebel against pastors and leaders (Deut. 17:12)
45. False prophets (Deut. 18:19–22)

46. Women who keep not their virginity until they are married (Deut. 22:13–21)
47. Parents who do not discipline their children, but honor them above God (1 Sam. 2:27–36)
48. Those who curse their rulers (Exod. 22:28; 1 Kings 2:8–9)
49. Those who teach rebellion against the Lord (Jer. 28:16–17)
50. Those who refuse to warn sinners (Ezek. 3:18–21)
51. Those who defile the Sabbath (Exod. 31:14; Num. 15:32–36)
52. Those who sacrifice human beings (Lev. 20:2)
53. Participants in seances and fortune-telling (Lev. 20:6)
54. Those involved in homosexual and lesbian relationships (Lev. 20:13)
55. Necromancers and fortune tellers (Lev. 20:27)
56. Those who blaspheme the Lord's name (Lev. 24:15–16)
57. Those who are carnally minded (Rom. 8:6)
58. Those who practice sodomy (Gen. 19:5–15, 24–25)
59. Rebellious children (Deut. 21:18–21)

Sin leads to curses. Accordingly, if a person continues to live in sin, deliverance will either not be possible, or happen only temporarily.

Before Jesus died on the cross for us, curses could not be broken. The curses went down the generations. Abraham had two sons Ishmael and Isaac. Hagar, Sarah's handmaid, bore Ishmael. Ishmael, the oldest, would normally be considered the proper heir. But because of Abraham's actions, the younger son, Isaac, received the blessings, thus breaking the normal rule. The effect went down the generations.

Twin sons were born to Isaac—Esau and Jacob. Again, the oldest son should have received the blessing, but circumstances left Jacob, the younger, as heir. In turn, Jacob had twelve sons, and the youngest, Joseph, became the inheritor of God's blessings (although all twelve later became the founders of the twelve tribes of Israel). Interestingly, in all three generations, the oldest offspring did not receive the inheritance as normally given.

The curse traveled further down the family line when Israel blessed Joseph's two sons. He gave his blessings to the younger of the two.

Even King David failed to escape the curses resulting from his adultery with Bathsheba and the murder of her husband, Uriah, although God forgave David. The prophet Nathan announced to David that despite God's forgiveness, *"the sword shall never depart from thine house"* (2 Sam. 12:10), and the child born to David and Bathsheba would die (2 Sam. 12:14). David's son, Absalom, killed his brother Ammon, who had raped his half-sister Tamar. Absalom later rebelled against David and died for it. Adonijah, another son of David, rebelled and gave his life for it also.

Jesus Served as Our Curse

The good news in that Jesus Christ served as a curse for you and me. Galatians 3:13 says,

> *Christ hath redeemed us from the curse of the law, being made a curse for us: for it is written, Cursed is every one that hangeth on a tree.*

Jesus Christ came to save the world, but we still need to claim Him as our Savior in order to be saved. He came to serve as a curse for us, but we still need to claim Him as our curse (Deut. 21:23). A positive confession of His power is required to break our curses.

Breaking Curses

We've found the following curse-breaking prayer to be simple and effective:

> Father, we come by the precious blood of our Savior Jesus Christ. We stand on the Word of God in Galations 3:13. Christ has redeemed us from the curse of the law, having served as a curse for us. For it is written, Cursed is everyone who hangs from a tree. We thank you, Lord Jesus, for serving as a curse for us, and we now claim your precious blood to take away all curses. By the authority given to me, I break the following curses: (state specific curses).

Immediately following a reading and breaking of those curses, call out the demon spirits:

> In the name of Jesus, and by the power of His blood, I command you to come out and leave. You, spirit of _____, come out! Spirit of _____, you come out in Jesus' name.

Go down the list of spirits. At first, the spirits may not manifest, but when you get to around the tenth spirit, you will notice people starting to scream, tremble, or hold their stomachs. As you continue, the spirits will start to leave.

Abominations in the Home and Person

Deuteronomy 7:26 says,

Neither shalt thou bring an abomination into thine house, lest thou be a cursed thing like it: but thou shalt utterly detest it, and thou shalt utterly abhor it; for it is a cursed thing.

Many Christians unwittingly bring abominations into the home. Statues of the Virgin Mary, different saints, Kwan Yin, Buddha, Shiva, carvings of tiki gods, books on the occult, fortune telling, stones and rocks from heathen temples, paintings of Roman and other gods, tarot cards, I-Ching books, ceramic and macramé depictions of frogs, owls, dragons, and other demonic objects are often found in Christian homes, posing as art objects and decorations. These cursed things bring strange diseases that doctors cannot diagnose, divorces, rebellious children, arguments, accidents, and oppression.

Demons will not leave until the cursed objects are taken out of the house or destroyed. In one case I dealt with, sleep eluded a woman because she had hung a black velvet painting of a dragon over her bed. Whenever she tried to sleep in her own room she found it almost impossible. However, when she traveled, she could sleep for twelve hours at a time. In another similar situation, a part Hawaiian woman tormented by nightmares and nocturnal spectral visitations finally gained peace by ridding her bedroom of a painting of the Hawaiian shark-god, her family's guardian spirit or "aumakua."

Rock-and-roll records, Dungeon and Dragon games, good-luck oriental dolls, samurai swords (the real kind), martial arts magic words (called "hus"), Buddhist altars, Aztec carvings, and souvenirs manufactured by Hare Krishna followers have all been the sources of curses. Often, seemingly innocent objects have been manufactured by Buddhists and followers of strange religions who pray over their products and "bless" them. Well-meaning friends pin good-luck charms on children or give away occultic crystals and wind chimes that are actually objects of Hindu, Buddhist, or Taoist worship.

I frequently find that certain jewelry may bring curses. Turquoise jewelry made by Pueblo Indians, Hindu copper bracelets, and other objects worn by a person could be of demonic origin. The makers of pieces of jewelry or furniture sometimes pray in order to place a spirit in those objects. In one case, a person wore a ring which depicted a goat's head—a symbol of Satan. In another, a ring featured a skull and crossbones. In still another case, a woman wore earrings of a crescent moon and stars. When these forbidden items were taken off, the demons left during deliverance.

Christians have reported cases of demonic invasion caused by Japanese dolls, puppets, Smurfs, cabbage patch dolls, and rock-and-roll records. I know a pastor who claims that he heard voices in his daughter's room one night and went in to check. He knew no one was at home. As he walked towards his daughter's room, he definitely heard voices. When he opened the door and switched the light on, he saw his daughter's doll collection staring at him. It so "spooked" him, that he took all the dolls outside and threw them into the rubbish can. After disposing of the dolls, his daughter's emotional problems lessened considerably. In another case, a member of our local church reported that his six-year-old child became frightened one night because her doll started talking to her.

I often come across rock-and-roll spirits that cause a person to dance, weave, and sing rock and roll songs during deliverance. Rock-and-roll music, especially "heavy metal," is tied to violence, murder, and drugs. I recall one young woman engaged in snapping her fingers and wild singing as we called out those spirits. Many hard rock groups spice their songs with praises to Satan and other similar demonic epithets. Some of these groups employ backmasking of tapes and records. Play some records or tapes backwards, and you hear praises to Satan. Some records contain lyrics designed to worship Satan or some demonic chant. Others sneak in words. For instance, if you take every tenth word in some lyrics and paste them together, they form some demonic statement which the human mind subconsciously picks up. Rock-and-roll records stored under the bed brought about sexual lust and masturbation in one reported case.

The crucifix with the body of Christ hanging from the cross is used in satanic rituals. Devil worshippers delight in seeing a dead Jesus on the cross. It is the resurrection they don't like. A close friend had a neighbor who claimed that his office was haunted. When he first moved in, he noticed a crucifix left there by the prior tenant. He vowed to rid the place of all such objects, in an attempt to cleanse the place. When he removed the crucifix and carried it into his car, it started to bleed. Drops of blood fell to the ground and on his automobile. He hurriedly threw it away. The place has not been "haunted" since.

Bleeding and crying statues make up part of the Babylonian lore, and many legends about statues speaking and becoming human can be found in heathen religions. Statues and idols are, of course, contrary to Christian teachings.

A man in his forties attended a talk I recently gave about deliverance. After the talk, he seemed very depressed and asked for help. He related that he could not understand a spiritual oppression that had set in five years previous. When pressed about his past, he suddenly recalled that five years prior he had played games such as Dungeons and Dragons constantly. Now, whenever someone mentioned the words "elf" or "sorcerer," his heart started beating faster and his body shook. Needless to say, those games had caused his spiritual oppression, and when they were repented for and destroyed, it lifted.

Pornographic materials are also demonic. Their presence in a home brings all kinds of problems with sexual lust, masturbation, and lack of mental concentration. They bring other manifestations besides sexual lust. It opens the gates to homosexuality, sexual fantasy, fornication, adultery, perversion, sexual uncleanness, incest, bestiality, and many other sexual spirits that belong within the ugly nest of sexual sins.

Children's cartoons and movies provide fertile ground for openings to satanic mind control. I was shocked one Saturday morning while observing my young son watching cartoons on television. Every cartoon seemed demonic. Smurfs, He-Man, monsters, demons, snakes, and other animals appeared as heroes. Movies such as Star Wars promote New Age ideas of a universal force and meditation. "The Force" is none other than the universal power or entity called "Tao" or the universal vibration or being which Buddhists, Hindus, and Taoists worship. Lifting up objects by the power of the mind as Luke Skywalker did is one of satanists' and martial artists' favorite lures. These movies increase men's desire for power and personal exaltation through self-improvement using meditation and other techniques.

Of course, we can become too legalistic. One cannot consider all representations of dragons, for instance, as cursed. The encyclopedia and other books sometimes contain pictures of oriental paintings or decorations which contain dragons or depictions of Buddha. It would be ridiculous to tear out every page which pictures a Buddhist temple or similar thing, although I generally consider all occult "how to" books definitely demonic. You need to ask the Holy Spirit about certain borderline items. Some people refuse to part with their objects, but expect God to bless the objects, while others anoint the object expecting to balance out any demonic influence. This is pure folly and will not bring about the desired results.

Tattoos

Leviticus 19:28 says, *"Ye shall not make any cuttings in your flesh for the dead, nor print any marks upon you: I am the LORD."* Body tattoos can bring curses. Tattooing involves the insertion of fine needles and the placing of dye into the punctures in order to form a pattern. One female Marine followed Navy traditions of obtaining a tattoo and vowing to "raise hell." Demons tormented this young woman day and night. She saw shadows and felt things grabbing her and carrying her while she slept. When the young woman renounced the tattoo and asked God to close all gates, the demons responded by attempting to scratch my eyes out. They screamed obscenities and spat at me. It took six people to hold her down, but the demons fled after a few moments.

Sorcerers often pass on their powers or demons through a tattoo on the body of a disciple or descendant. Small wonder that God forbade the Israelites to mark their bodies in such a fashion.

Women sometimes ask me about cosmetic tattooing where lip color and eye shadow are tattooed in permanently. I don't know the answer to that one, although it would seem that once you know that the Bible warns about disfiguring your body or placing marks on it, marking your body for cosmetic purposes would be sinful. If you are unsure and do it anyway, it is without faith and any-

cosmetic purposes would be sinful. If you are unsure and do it anyway, it is without faith and anything done without faith is sin. *"And he that doubteth is damned...for whatsoever is not of faith is sin"* (Rom. 14:23).

Clean Dwellings

Demons may persist in inhabiting a dwelling even after the practice of worship to them is discontinued. In one case, a woman worshipped the Chinese goddess Kwan Yin for over 40 years. She burned incense twice a day and offered food and drink daily. Some family members regularly assisted her out of respect, although most were Christians. Even after repeated deliverance sessions, complete release evaded them. The occupants threw away all paraphernalia of demon worship, including altars and incense. Nevertheless, the house remained oppressed.

It was not until I gave the house a Christian blessing and cleansing that complete release took place. During the cleansing ceremony, one of the occupants started to shake, and demons started to manifest. The demons cried out, "Why, oh why, did you have to cleanse this house? I can't stand it, it's too clean." They left.

We normally use the following procedure to cleanse a dwelling:

- A group of believers should pray for the house at least one day before gathering at the house. Ask God to send his angels in advance to clean out the premises. Claim the power of the blood of Jesus over the house. In a number of cases, the house-holders reported that the house felt clean the very same day the saints offered prayers for the house, and the householder never even knew about the prayers.

- Conduct a simple Holy Communion service at the house with most, or preferably all, members of the family or occupants of the dwelling. Bring them to a point of forgiveness between and among each member. You can use bread, crackers, or similar available items to serve as bread. You can also use wine, grape juice, or even water.

- Walk the entire perimeter of the land, if it is a house, and claim the lot for the kingdom of God. For example, "Everywhere that my foot treads or where my finger points, I claim for the kingdom of God, and I command all unclean spirits to leave in the name of Jesus."

- Take a vial of oil (any kind will do, although I usually carry my own olive oil), ask God to let it represent the blood of Jesus, and bless it with His power and authority. Anoint each doorway and window with the oil by dabbing the sides and the tops. Ask God to place an invisible shield around the house and over each window and door. Pray that God will post an angel at each opening and surround the house in time of need. Once, as we prayed for the angels, the demons started pointing at angels and screaming, "Who sent the angels?" "Why are they here?" "There are so many." "They're so big." "I can't stay." "The angels are coming with chains to get me."

- As you walk around the house, be sensitive to the Holy Spirit. You will often feel the presence of evil spirits by the pressing down on your spirit or a "knowing." Frequently, if your hair stands up, that spot is infested. Such manifestations are confirmed time and time again by the occupants of the house.

- Break all curses on the house and its inhabitants. Warn the inhabitants that continued sinful conduct will invite the demons back into the premises and into their lives with more power than they had before.

Unforgiveness

One of the most insidious areas of curses is unforgiveness. In Matthew 18:23–35, Jesus tells his disciples of the servant whose lord forgave the servant a huge debt of over $52,800,000 by modern standards. The same servant went out and found a fellow servant who owed him $44, took him by the throat, and commanded the fellow servant to pay him. When the fellow servant could not pay, the first servant cast him into prison. When his lord found out, he said,

> *"O thou wicked servant, I forgave thee all that debt, because thou desiredst me: shouldest not thou also have had compassion on thy fellowservant, even as I had pity on thee?" And his lord was wroth, and delivered him to the tormentors, till he should pay all that was due unto him.* (Matt. 18:32–34)

Jesus then said, *"So likewise shall my heavenly father do also unto you, if ye from your hearts forgive not every one his brother their trespasses"*

(Matt. 18:35). One of the meanings of the word "tormentors" is "demons."

Forgiveness is an important key to setting captives free. Demons often resist and refuse to come out, even after heavy bombardment. As soon as the person forgives, the demons flee. Often, the demons cry out, "Why did you make her forgive her father? Now we have to go."

In one case we bombarded spirits of fear for perhaps thirty minutes without success, even though the demons moaned and groaned from the persistent attack. The spirits kept insisting that they had a right to stay. Finally, the pastor walked by and mentioned that God had just shown him that the woman had to forgive her father and uncle. We commanded the spirits to go back down and allow the woman to surface. When the woman acknowledged that Jesus is Lord (spirits usually cannot say it), we told her what God had said. She immediately started to weep, "I can't. I hate them." Gradually, however, we led her through a prayer asking Jesus to give her a heart of forgiveness. She mentally wanted to forgive but her heart did not allow her. When the woman finally said, "I forgive them" from her heart, we immediately declared to the demons, "You heard that, demon, she forgave her father and uncle. You come out in the name of Jesus." The demons came out immediately.

Unforgiveness is indeed a hated sin in God's eyes, and it is also a strong legal ground for Satan. Remember, if you don't forgive others their sins against you, God will not forgive you your sins against Him. Thus, the curses derived from your sins continue to work in your life. Over and over again, Jesus teaches us to forgive others. There is no sense sacrificing to God if you have anything against your brother (Matt. 5:22–25). Before you can take the splinter out of your brother's eye, take the mote out of your own (Matt. 7:4–5).

When counseling, you need to explain forgiveness in detail. God will not deliver a person until the person reaches a place of humility and repentance. When I first entered into deliverance, I submitted six consecutive times with no results. I began to feel that God didn't love me. After each failure, workers told me to go home and get rid of all my occultic books and idols and ask God to forgive me for my specific sins. After each "failure," I tore apart my house looking for books, carvings, and other occultic paraphernalia. Finally, after the sixth attempt, I was in desperate straits. As I groaned and cried out to God early the next morning, God began to show me some sinful things I did years before becoming a Christian. He actually gave me visions of events long ago forgotten and people not seen for many years. God made me realize how ugly all forms of sin are to Him, even those done "innocently" or out of youthful folly.

The very evening after God showed me those sins, I went through a wonderful deliverance session. You see, deliverance always works, but deliverance remains within God's providence and timing. It is the same with healing. Very often, God wants more from the person before blessing him or her.

There is simply no excuse for unforgiveness. It is a sin. Many people absolutely refuse to forgive.

Someone hurt them, so their pride smolders in self-righteousness and resentment. They subsequently dedicate their lives to revenge, self-pity, and bitterness. They find themselves in all kinds of torment and physical problems—heart trouble, cancer, hypertension, kidney failures, diabetes, et cetera, and they still refuse to forgive. Some wear all of the trespasses people ever did to them on their sleeves. It becomes almost a badge of heroism, like a Purple Heart medal given to the wounded in battle. "Tell me your troubles, and I'll tell you mine." They love to put this sad "poor me" face on and cry on your shoulders for hours. They wring their hands and weep profusely, but they don't want to change. They measure their friends by how much sympathy each one gives. They love their pity parties and righteous indignation.

Asking them to give up their bitterness is akin to asking them to cut off their right arms. They would rather die to be right, and often they do. They seek the advice of believers but don't want to give up their hatred. They often end up being manic depressives or schizophrenics. Unforgiveness is disobedience and rebellion against God.

A general prayer asking for forgiveness or forgiving others won't suffice. Often people pray, "I forgive my mother for everything she has ever done to me." Sometimes it's "I forgive everybody that ever sinned against me." It is not sufficient. One needs to get before the Lord and bare his heart. God wants a washing from the inside, not just the outside. Your mind can say it, but your heart can remain unaffected and hard. Be specific.

Soul Ties

> *And it came to pass, when he had made an*
> *end of speaking unto Saul, that the soul of*
> *Jonathan was knit with the soul of David,*
> *and Jonathan loved him as his own soul.*
>
> (1 Sam. 18:1)

The souls of men and women also knit together with negative repercussions. A domineering mother's soul knitted to her son's, and he ended up in an insane asylum suffering from schizophrenia. When the woman cut the spiritual umbilical cord and cast it off, the son recovered instantly and several days later left the asylum normal (McAll 7–9). Manipulation and control by another person may create negative soul ties.

Often the souls of ex-lovers knit together, even though they no longer see each other. They may marry others, but they continue to be tormented by thoughts of the former lover. Strange circumstances may bring them together, and they bump into each other at unlikely times and places. Even if their relationship ended on a sour note, they often think of, fantasize about, and lust for each other. Their soul ties need to be broken and cast off.

One wife in our church kept bumping into an ex-lover, although neither party consciously arranged it. Demons tormented her constantly with lustful fantasy thoughts and frustration. She found herself unable to fully love her husband, a wonderful Christian brother. Soon her moodiness prevented her from growing in God, despite every effort on her part.

When she finally broke the soul ties, the demons tormenting her left, and she grew daily in the Lord. With the oppression and guilt gone, her relationships with her husband and others flourished.

Other negative ties include homosexual partners, former bosses, teachers, employers, employees, parents, siblings, relatives, or anyone who played a dominant part in your life at some point. Sexual partners can pass multitudes of spirits on through sex.

If demons seem to get stronger during a session, someone in the room could have spirits who feed the demons in the person being delivered. You need to cut soul ties between those people and ask God to place a shield around the person so that no other spirits can feed and give strength to the person's demons. Sometimes you may need to physically separate people such as buddies, spouses, boyfriends and girlfriends, or parents and children.

In one such case, after bombarding martial arts spirits of Ki or Chi, the spirits started calling another person in the room by name. At first, we thought the person being delivered was calling because he felt that the second person could help cast out the demons. As the second person walked toward the first, the demons started to become stronger. (I do not mean to imply that distance affects a demon's strength.) Needless to say, when we put a shield around him, cut soul ties, and ushered the second person out of sight, the spirits gave up and left.

Witchcraft creates heavy negative soul ties. In addition, the soul can be fragmented and destroyed piecemeal. Satan steals away fragments of the soul so that the victim never feels complete or at peace. Somehow, he feels something missing in his life, and he doesn't know what.

In one case, a woman's parents dedicated her to Satan as an infant, so she never felt completely at peace with herself although she faithfully walked with Jesus and attended church regularly. She didn't even know about the dedication until the Holy Spirit showed her. In another situation I worked with, a good friend of the troubled person practiced witchcraft. The troubled person often dreamt of the friend and at times even heard the friend calling her, although she was alone. Though they had not talked to each other in person for a number of years, the tormented person's thoughts were being controlled by her friend.

We asked God to send as many angels as necessary to recover the fragments of her soul, put them back in proper order, and quicken and restore them to her. Something literally snapped in her, and she suddenly felt complete and whole for the first time since she could recall. Her mind became clear and she felt alive.

> *Thus saith the Lord GOD; Woe to the women that sew pillows to all armholes, and make kerchiefs upon the head of every stature to hunt souls! Will ye hunt the souls of my people, and will ye save the souls alive that come unto you? And will ye pollute me among my people for handfuls of barley and for pieces of bread, to slay the souls that should not die, and to save the souls alive that should not*

93

*live, by your lying to my people that hear your
lies? Wherefore thus saith the Lord GOD; Behold, I am against your pillows, wherewith ye
there hunt the souls to make them fly, and I
will tear them from your arms, and will let
the souls go, even the souls that ye hunt to
make them fly. Your kerchiefs also will I tear,
and deliver my people out of your hand, and
they shall be no more in your hand to be
hunted; and ye shall know that I am the
LORD.* (Ezek. 13:18–22)

Names

Sometimes, naming a person after some ancestor will form a soul tie with that person. Hawaiians
love to name their children after gods, kahunas, or
famous ancestors. Orientals name their children
after famous people, ancestors, or priests. They take
their children to the Shinto or Buddhist temple and
dedicate them to the gods or goddesses. Because of
the name and/or dedication, a soul tie is created.

Names are important to God. You may recall
that God changed the name of Abram to Abraham
(Gen. 17:5), and Jacob to Israel (Gen. 32:28). In
those days, an individual's name was significant
inasmuch as it reflected either character or destiny.
When the two sons of Eli were killed and Eli broke
his neck and died, Eli's daughter-in-law named her
newborn son Ichabod, meaning "the glory of the
Lord is gone."

In the book of Revelation, God promised that
He would give each overcomer a new name written

on a white stone (Rev. 2:17). God also promised to write on the forehead of each overcomer the secret name of God, the name of the city of God, and the new name given to the Lord Jesus (Rev. 3:12).

Unfortunately, names can create a negative bond, so we need to break demonic vows and ties that are associated with names.

Involvement in the Occult

Involvement in the occult, whether it is innocent or otherwise, can bring about strong curses. Not only that, but scary nocturnal visitors, ghostly apparitions, voices, and bizarre happenings may start to occur in a person's life as he or she becomes involved in the occult.

Some feel oppressed and sense a dark presence. Others begin to hear voices at night and even during the day. The voices often start out sweet and charming but end up as screams full of rough, filthy, blasphemous words. Some see things at night—a shadow of a head, hands, or legs; forms floating around; forms disappearing around corners; things moving around without human hands; or objects simply disappearing.

Some report loud voices at night and feel their spirits leaving the bodies in levitation or astral projection without effort and against their wills. A few report nightmares of being forced into perverted sex with a half-goat, half-man beast, while other spirits look on and cheer. They wake up physically bruised and exhausted. Nightly visitations leave them tired and desperate.

Strange Religions

All strange religions are demonic in origin. Most seem quite innocent while a few are overtly satanic. On one end of the spectrum is satanism, with human sacrifice and eerie rituals involving Satan himself, witches, and warlocks. On the other end are seemingly innocuous religions such as Buddhism, Hinduism, Mormonism, Scientology, Christian Scientist, Unity, and similar Christian cults. In between are religions such as Santerias, Voodoo, Kahuna, Taoism, Shintoism, Roman Catholicism, New Age, and a wide array of native religions from the South Pacific, Africa, Central America, Europe, and other parts of the world. Every area of the world has its own brand of indigenous demon worship. All involve the occult in one form or other.

Other pseudo-religious activities which can bring a person into occult bondage include psychic healing, Free Masonry, and secret societies. Certain boy scout organizations engage in American Indian religion by assigning Indian guides or warriors to each scout.

Other occult activities that bring curses are: use of ouija boards, participation in seances, fortune-telling, tarot cards, palm reading, I Ching, crystals, 8–balls, astrology, dousing, face reading, consulting psychics, holistic healing, acupuncture, martial arts, foreign religions, Dungeons and Dragons, voodoo, folk superstitions, Indian sorcery, folk healing using "good" spirits, chants and rituals, occultic music, and also plain old witchcraft. Athletes and gamblers use magic charms and relics for good luck, such as carrying a rabbit's foot for success. These all bring demonic invasion, curses, and usually some sickness.

Holistic healing, acupuncture, martial arts, Dungeons and Dragons, children's cartoons, movies, and TV shows open wide gates for satanic invasion. In the church itself, some inner healing methods may introduce shamanistic techniques such as visualization, focusing, and mental processing. Witchcraft has included visioning and imaging for centuries. The New Age movement also uses imaging and focusing constantly. Anyone who has ever been involved in occult activities will instantly recognize certain Christian inner-healing techniques that have their origins in the occult.

Any delving into fortune-telling, ouija boards, crystals, good luck charms, I Ching, 8 ball, astrology, tarot cards, palm reading, seances, and similar occultic activities opens doors for evil spirits. The results may not be immediate but will eventually enslave a person. In the end times, Satan will control the minds and bodies of men and women. He set the stage by introducing the occult to children through cartoons, movies, and toys. Many cartoons and movies feature occultic themes in a deceptive manner. Cartoon characters such as space monsters, friendly Smurfs, and others prepare people for the acceptance of demons. Not all demons seem ugly. They can appear as alluring people and heroes. Children will associate demons with friendly beings such as E.T. and the elves working for Santa Claus. The public is slowly being desensitized to the presence of evil spirits.

Spirit Guides

Many Christians picked up demonic spirit guides through vows and dedications. Often, guides are assigned to a person by a martial arts instructor, hula instructor, drum teacher, or as part of a religion. The Roman Catholics often name children after saints and sometimes dedicate them to certain saints and the Virgin Mary. The saints and the Virgin Mary are demons that become demonic spirit guides.

People who were deeply engaged in fortune-telling such as reading palms, astrology, tarot cards, and tea leaves, often received from their instructors spirit guides to "help them." Some forms of psychic healing involve supposedly "good" spirits. Reiki healing and other similar forms of miracle healing found in Mexico and the Philippines are sleight of hand tricks, but sometimes they are real. People may engage in such activities with good intentions, but even so, they are deceived.

Martial arts instructors commonly ask ancient warrior gods to go into an individual to help that person develop his fighting skills or to protect him. Each has his own patron gods. Students may discover later that these spirit guides are real.

Vows and Dedications

Parents often make vows and dedicate their children to a particular god or goddess. Orientals, and Roman Catholics especially, include this in their traditions. Sometimes, it is a boy scout or girl scout dedication to some American Indian guide spirit, a vow and dedication to Freemasonry, or some secret society's patron saint or god.

These vows give evil spirits the right to enter into a person's life. The demon will actually claim that person's soul, even though he or she has become a Christian. Sometimes a saint will report feelings that he is not saved or dreams about some strange god beckoning them. Vows and dedications must be renounced and broken by the person prayed for.

Psychic Heredity

Psychic inheritance includes the ability to tell fortunes including the disaster or death of someone, to find things, to predict happenings, and to have visions and dreams that are occultic in nature. Some inherit spirit guides, often a dead ancestor. Some have been appointed as successor to an ancestor who was a noted psychic, fortune-teller, or sorcerer.

In one particular case, a young Christian woman began to be tormented at night with specters, shadows, and voices. Unseen hands grabbed her, and many weird things began to happen to her. God revealed that a living aunt of hers practiced witchcraft, and the aunt had designated the young woman as her successor. We broke soul ties with her aunt, and she renounced the occult out loud. We rebuked the demons and called them out. Over a period of time, the woman found release from her captivity.

Roman Catholicism

Ex-Roman Catholics often suffer from witchcraft curses brought about through worship of the Virgin Mary or different saints. Worship of saints is a form of necromancy, and the real virgin Mary may be in heaven while a demon counterfeiting her is demanding worship from humans on earth. The Virgin Mary and various saints are commonly worshipped along with heathen gods in a kind of "chopsuey" or mixture of Christianity and pagan religions. Fortune-telling and supernatural healing through native folklore are part of the Roman Catholic religion.

The problem with Roman Catholicism is its practice of absorbing native religions into the church by adopting pagan customs and rites. Puerto Rican people mix Roman Catholicism with Santerias, voodoo, and other native religions.

When I was in the Philippines, I came across a young man who had been a Roman Catholic. He had been a very devout and well-meaning Catholic, even having gone so far as to allow himself to be nailed to a cross to show his penance. As the men whipped him, he had cried out, "Harder, you hit me like girls, like queers!" He almost died while hanging from the cross, and his devotion was unquestioned.

As we were singing and praising God during a service, the young man bent over in pain as spirits manifested in his belly. We pulled him aside and began administering deliverance. Many demons of Roman Catholicism came out, such as Mariolatry (excessive veneraton for Jesus' earthly mother), The

Crucifix, Lying Demons, Penance, Purgatory, Confession Box, False Doctrine, The One True Church, Fear of Priests, and Virgin Mary.

In the early fourth century, the Roman Empire adopted Christianity as the official state religion. In its zeal to convert the heathen element of the Empire to Christianity, the Empire compromised Christianity by allowing the pagans to merely change the names of their demonic deities to the names of various saints. The pagans kept on worshipping their demonic deities in the name of Christianity.

Hundreds of years later, Satan induced the Roman Catholic Church to adopt the worship of the mother-child deity of Babylon. All Babylonian religions worship a mother-child. Aemiramis and Tammuz became the Virgin Mary and Baby Jesus. Osiris Horis, and Isis became Father, Son, and Mary. The Bible calls this ugly spirit the virgin, daughter of Babylon (Isa. 47:1). It also calls her the lady of kingdoms (Isa. 47:5), virgin, daughter of Egypt (Jer 46:11), and queen of heaven (Jer. 44:17–19). Unfortunately, a full treatment of the subject cannot be handled in this book. For a powerful view on this subject, read *The Two Babylons or the Papal Worship* written by Bishop Hislop and *Babylon Mystery Religion* by Ralph Woodrow.

Most Roman Catholics are lovely people who are sincere and devoted about their faith. I love them and have delivered many from demonic bondage. Their religion as practiced today is a mixture of truth and lies, Christianity and heathenism; unfortunately, deception runs deep.

Drugs

Drugs play an important part in witchcraft. The "mystery cup of iniquity" refers to the ancient Chaldean rite of offering a golden cup filled with mind altering drugs to initiates of the Babylonian religion. (See Revelation 17:4.) Such drugs brought about a hallucinatory state through which the partaker could see into the spirit world and experience things unknown to the human conscience. These "spiritual" experiences convinced practitioners that they had seen gods. Much the same happens today with our youth. Drug experiences convince them of the mysterious power behind drugs and that they have a higher level of consciousness. Heavy bondage ensues. Drug users often find themselves hearing voices because they have opened a door for demonic entry.

Satyr

When a person voluntarily (and sometimes involuntarily) involves himself or herself in witchcraft, his or her name ends up in the goat's (Sater's) Book of Death, the counterfeit of the Lamb's Book of Life.

As mentioned earlier, when praying against witchcraft spirits, we occasionally see a half-goat, half-man spirit. We know him as Satyr, Pan, Faun, Camut, or Kammutz. In one case, the beast-man appeared with a vest and a pair of gold-rimmed spectacles and kept looking down into a large book. When you see this spirit, it evidences heavy occult involvement by the person or his forefathers. Witchcraft must be absolutely renounced, and the person must repent and ask forgiveness. His or her dwelling must be cleansed and blessed. All abominations or traces of witchcraft must be destroyed, including jewelry with witchcraft signs. Not so coincidentally, many people with a witchcraft spirit love to wear rings with the head of a goat, earrings with the crescent moon and star, or other jewelry with occultic objects, signs, and symbols.

The Passive Mind

Not so obvious is the occultic connection with religions such as Buddhism and Hinduism. The New Age movement is fraught with danger having as its core Zen Buddhism, Hinduism, Taoism, Shamanism, and Roman Catholicism. The New Age movement is deceptively good and innocent from the outside, but its core is truly demonic. Mental processes, including meditation, come directly from Hinduism and Buddhism and open wide the gates to one's body and soul. Those who practice meditation and the like interpret their impending demonic manifestations as godly visions. Demonic religions use passivity of the mind and body to open the gates to evil spirits.

Deliverance workers know quite well that a passive mind and body invites spirits by surrendering the normal processes to outside forces. "Jesus chanting" and "waiting on God" sessions, both of which use blanking out techniques, invite evil spirits instead of the Holy Spirit. For a more thorough treatment of passivity, read Jessie Penn-Lewis's excellent book entitled *War on the Saints*.

Holistic Healing

Holistic healing in its many forms, including Reiki and psychic healing, remains purely demonic. These forms have their origins in Buddhism and other Eastern religions. They may use the Lord's prayer and the name of Jesus, but it works with or without mention of Jesus' name. The same holds true with other forms of healing such as visualization used by Shamans. Some "Christian inner healing" proves to be no different than what the Buddhists and witch doctors use around the world. Kahunas and American Indian sorcerers have employed visioning, imaging, and focusing techniques for centuries.

It works, but the evil sources and origins make such techniques part of witchcraft. Johanna Michaelson's book entitled *The Beautiful Side of Evil* provides an excellent treatise on the subject of psychic healing. Hunt and Mahon's book entitled *The Seduction of Christianity* gives an eye-opening exposé of inner healing in the Christian church. Not all forms of inner healing are occultic, but we do need to be very careful.

In their zeal or desire to get "one up" on the competition, many chiropractors and some medical doctors adopt holistic healing techniques without knowing anything about the true source of their newly discovered powers. Thus, people frequently conclude that all supernatural miracles come from

God. How foolish they are! The Word of God clearly states:

> *For Satan himself is transformed into an angel of light. Therefore it is no great thing if his ministers also be transformed as the ministers of righteousnes.* (2 Cor. 11:14–15)

The fact that a person does "good" things does not automatically mean they are serving God.

EST, PSI, Gestalt, Silva Mind Control, Rolfing, New Age, Transcendental Meditation, birthing therapy, and a slew of modern motivational and mind-altering disciplines have similar occultic origins. They represent Satan's tremendous ability to deceive even the very elect, if it were possible. I've had to deliver many young people from bondage caused by such self-improvement courses. As you can see, Satan's web is extremely extensive, and his snares are countless.

Sexual Sins

In these end times, Satan is saturating the world with things of the flesh. He knows that sexual sins are particularly despised by God. Leviticus eighteen lists some of the sexual sins God abhors. Among them we find homosexuality, sexual promiscuity, fornication, adultery, bestiality, sodomy, incest, and general sexual lust. Extremely heavy bondage often follows sexual sins.

The world is already full of sexual lust and opportunity. It's difficult to watch television without seeing sexually explicit commercials, shows, music videos, and movies. They all promote sexual promiscuity. Sexual lust brings man down to the level of the brute beast nature of Jude and 2 Peter 2:12–15. As the world moves deeper into darkness, men will become like animals—lawless, full of insatiable lusts, and completely overcome by the flesh.

The Women's Liberation movement brought the sexual revolution to new heights, and many women now aggressively seek out sexual partners. Morality is not an issue. Individual freedom and the U.S. Constitution take priority over holiness and the Bible. Sexually aggressive men and women make it difficult to remain celibate or pure. Adultery among both husbands and wives is common today. All kinds of sexual entertainment and experimentation have increased among most ages and levels of society. People no longer view sexual uncleanliness as sin, and few refuse to indulge in it. America has become a veritable Sodom and Gomorrah.

Before lasting deliverance can be achieved, the person needs to renounce sexual sins and repent. Failure to desire change in sexual areas will keep that person in bondage. Sexual lust represents a difficult area in deliverance because of the ample opportunities available to indulge. The person who desires to be rid of sexual lust must realize the dangers of allowing his or her eyes to drink in what the world offers. The knowledge of how God views the ugliness of sexual sins and the heartfelt desire to avoid future sins of sex must burn in a person's soul, the mind must be changed, and discipline applied.

If a person desires only temporary relief, he will not achieve permanent deliverance. Some want to control their lusts when they cannot satisfy them, yet when opportunity arises to indulge, they don't mind them. They look at sexual fantasy as harmless entertainment for the mind and body. Once, a church member had a dream in which he found himself in a park-like area with gazebos and pretty shrubs with fruits that looked like cheese. Tiny cows were running around like little puppies, grabbing the cheese and then running away, teasing the dreamer. The dreamer remembered remarking that the miniature cows were "so cute" and friendly, playing tag with him and running around. The next scene was a sexual scene.

The Lord showed us that the cute miniature cows represented sexual fantasies which occupied much of the dreamer's thoughts. He never considered lustful fantasies to be anything but harmless entertainment—like cuddly, little puppies playing tag. But these tiny cows were dangerous. They stole away the cheese—the blessings of life, because they prevented the dreamer from moving forward and growing in God. They seem harmless but nevertheless rob and steal away the fruits of life.

It takes real effort to conquer spirits of lust. One cannot blame evil spirits for every affliction. The spirits may leave, but the habits and choices remain. The human will becomes the prime target. No person can claim true maturity in Christ without discipline, and sexual lust remains a supreme test of man's will. As long as a person indulges in sexual uncleanness, Satan's legal right to torment remains. I've cast out many sex spirits only to find the same ones back again because the saint went back to his old habits and desires.

Religious and Cultural Ties

In the section on occult involvement, we discussed occult curses derived from strange religions. However, Christians can also unwittingly involve themselves in dangerous activities through tradition.

Many Christians indulge in traditions and customs that are derived from heathen (satanic) religions. For instance, most daily newspapers feature a column on astrology or horoscopes. Astrology originated from the Chaldeans, Babylon's ruling tribe (Isa. 47:13). Star-gazing is a sign of heathenism (Jer. 10:2). Yet, Christians participate in these dangerous occultic activities with relish.

Card playing comes out of fortune-telling practices during the Middle Ages. In fact, the characters jack, king, queen, and joker come directly from tarot cards. Some fortune tellers even use regular decks of playing cards. In addition, many Christians love gambling and the bright lights of Las Vegas, Reno, or some other favorite gambling spot.

Halloween is another observance that comes directly out of Satan worship. On this day, human sacrifices occur around the world, according to a number of ex-satanists. Halloween originally represented the witches' answer to All Saints' Day observed annually by the Christian church on

November 1. Witches retaliated by having their Witches' Day on the eve of All Saints' Day. Ironically, more Christians now observe the witches' holiday than All Saints' Day, and many churches help the witches celebrate their most important holiday by holding Halloween parties.

There was an incident where a very realistic werewolf mask resulted in a wolf spirit entering the wearer. During a deliverance, the wolf surfaced and started howling. We discovered that the mask was kept in the house and used on Halloween night each year. The mask actually belonged to a brother who lived in the same house. It was so realistic and scary that one had to react to it. According to Elaine Lee and Rebecca Brown, werewolves actually exist in Satan's realm. He uses them to keep order among satanists.

Many Christian Orientals continue to burn fire-crackers and observe Buddhist or Taoist holidays. The practice of taking food to graves on certain days ("Bi Sun") and the burning of incense to ancestors should be discontinued. I find entire households under bondage to demons because of the curses brought about by these "strange fires" (Lev. 10:1–2; Num. 26:61). In many cases, a parent in the same household may continue to be a Buddhist and insist that his or her altar be untouched. Of course, this presents a difficult situation, and one should appeal to God to open the parent's eyes and to place a shield around the believer and the room he or she sleeps in.

The substitution of the name Jesus for Shiva, Buddha, or any other demon fails to change the origin or the bondage it brings. We sometimes observe Christians who "Jesus chant" and "wait upon God" in the lotus position, concentrating on their "third eye." Their flippant excuses are that all spiritual laws were created by God, that the enemy uses God's spiritual laws, and that Christians have a right to use these laws also. That is extremely naïve. If the Bible does not clearly outline the use of these "laws" we should not use them. Further, it is akin to saying that we have a right to anything used by the occult. God clearly admonishes us not to follow heathen customs (Jer. 10:2).

Some Christian traditions are definitely Babylonian in origin. Easter derives its origin from Ishtar's spring festival of fertility that takes place in early April. The original word in the Bible was "Passover," but the English translators picked up the word "Easter" which crawled into the Bible because of the invasion of heathen customs up to that time. Medieval satanists worshipped Ishtar as the Babylonian goddess of witchcraft and fertility. Colored eggs, bunnies, and hot-cross buns (cakes to the Queen of Heaven in Jeremiah 44:17–19) were Ishtar's signs.

The use of prayer beads by the Hindus and Buddhists have ended up being called the Rosary. Monks and nuns came from the Hindu and Buddhist religions which already existed around 500 B.C. Even their clothing and bald heads are similar.

Christmas trees continue to fascinate Christians all around the world. The following Scripture in Jeremiah seems to explicitly prohibit this modern-day practice:

Thus saith the LORD, Learn not the way of the heathen, and be not dismayed at the signs of heaven; for the heathen are dismayed at them. For the customs of the people are vain: for one cutteth a tree out of the forest, the work of the hands of the workman, with the ax. They deck it with silver and gold; they fasten it with nails and with hammers, that it move not. They are upright as the palm tree, but speak not: they must needs be borne, because they cannot go. (Jer. 10:2–5)

These signs represent Tammuz, the sun god mentioned in Ezekiel 8:14. The Bible prophesies that Tammuz, the Babylonian sun god, the son of Ishtar (Semiramis) would be worshipped by God's own priests and church in the end times. The Babylonians were dismayed at the signs of heaven; they originated astrology. Therefore, Jeremiah chapter ten refers to the Babylonians. Yule logs and mistletoe also come from Druid and Tammuz worship practices.

Christians have adopted many signs, symbols, and objects which originated in heathen or Satan worship rites.

I'm not saying that these signs should be the exclusive property of the kingdom of darkness. But, we need to know where they come from. So many Christian observances and customs as they are mentioned in the Word of God indicate heathen intrusion. They become stumbling blocks and erode our liberty in the Holy Spirit. No wonder God commands us not to make any graven images.

God has not changed. The Word says, *"I change not"* (Mal. 3:6), and *"Jesus Christ the same yesterday, and to day, and for ever* (Heb. 13:8). Recall that in Leviticus 10:1–2 and Numbers 26:61, Aaron's two sons, Nadab and Abihu, died because they offered strange fire before the Lord. It does not matter how enthusiastic or well-meaning you are. Nadab and Abihu may not have realized how precise and careful they were required to be in the presence of God. The Bible does not say what the strange fire was. If what you are involved in is not of God, then it is strange fire.

Hexes

People can intentionally or unintentionally curse or hex people. Witches make direct and intentional attacks on Christians and others. Satan often sends a "Bride of Satan" to infiltrate churches and send hexes against its members. Friends and family sometimes unintentionally open people up to demonic attack through innocent psychic prayers, dedications, or vows made to Buddha, Kwan Yin, Mother Kali, the Virgin Mary, et cetera.

In one case, a Christian woman worked in the same office with a known witch. When the Christian got into an office argument with the witch, the witch apparently placed a hex on the Christian woman's family. Her husband and two young children got dizzy and sick. We quickly recognized it as a hex. We prayed and claimed the blood of Jesus and asked God to break the curses and send the hexes back to the sender. When the woman returned to the office after lunch, the witch had been taken to the hospital after falling over from dizzy spells.

A number of Christians object to reversing curses, based on the Scriptures that say we should bless those who curse us. On the other hand, some noted deliverance workers, such as Win Worley, advocate sending curses back to whoever sent them.

Many Christians inadvertently get involved in psychic prayers by asking God to make somebody fall in love with them, force someone to do something against his will, or change another person's mind about a matter. These manipulative prayers suggest witchcraft. Witchcraft is defined as "manipulation of others," especially through chants, prayers, potions, and drugs. We need to be careful how we petition God, because we sometimes pray amiss.

How do you break hexes? Simply break them in the name of our Lord Jesus Christ and by the power of His blood. We have been given all authority to tread on serpents and scorpions and over all powers of the enemy (Luke 10:19).

In Summary

The first step in casting out demons is taking away their legal rights. Jesus often said, "Thy sins be forgiven" when healing people. God's forgiveness broke curses over that person, which enabled healing (Matt. 9:2; Mark 2:5; Luke 5:20; Luke 7:48). Deal with curses first and then command the demons to leave. Eliminating curses may take a period of time if there are many; however, you don't have to break every single curse in order to cast out demons. You need to break those which apply to the demons you are confronting.

Chapter Five

Knowledge
and
Discernment

Pure discernment of spirits is a gift from God, according to first Corinthians chapter twelve verse ten. Pray for it.

Some Christians see spirits in a bodily form such as black or white monkey-like creatures on the backs of people, clinging to their heads, coming out of people, or walking around. While being delivered, some people, see demons leering at them. A few see demons inside of their bodies. Others see creatures of every shape and size coming and going, but "seeing" remains relatively rare. I've never personally seen these spirits with open eyes. I've read accounts of people such as Ken Hagin, who occasionally observes these demons through his spiritual eyes as if looking directly at them with natural eyes.

Discernment—a Knowing

What is more important than seeing spirits is having the ability to discern these spirits. Sometimes, discernment is just a knowing. You just know that you know—like a word of knowledge or a perception. You look at a person and immediately you know.

Ways of Knowing

Occasionally in the heat of deliverance, the Holy Spirit simply speaks the name of the evil spirit out loud. Often, you think that one of the other workers spoke. Invariably, when you repeat the name that the Holy Spirit gave you, the demons will scream angrily, "Who told you?" They must come out then. Demons sometimes refuse to come out until you call them by name, although it's mostly a stalling technique. Some say, "I don't have to come out!" You ask them, "Why, demon? Speak up." They will reply, "You haven't said my name." When this happens and you don't have discernment, command the demon to give his name. If you persist, he must divulge his name. In the majority of cases, however, naming the spirit is not necessary.

Sometimes the Holy Spirit places a thought or picture in your mind, and you know what spirit it is. For instance, a lock of hair, snake, a spider with a woman's face covered with heavy makeup, or a very young naked girl indicates the virgin daughter of Babylon—Jezebel again. The Spirit frequently uses Bible verses to reveal spirits.

The Holy Spirit also uses visions and dreams to reveal the presence of certain spirits. These dreams can be given to the person himself or others in the church. The spirit can also be seen through the fruits in the person's life. Difficulties in marriage, problems with alcohol, drugs, or relationships clearly show what spirits are working in the person.

During a deliverance, your mind must be in concert with the Holy Spirit who places thoughts, impressions, and pictures in rapid order in your mind. As you learn how to respond to them, you will be able to separate what is from the Spirit and what is from your own mind. Hebrews 5:14 says, "*But strong meat belongeth to them that are of full age, even those who by reason of use have their senses exercised to discern both good and evil.*" In the beginning, you go by "hit and miss," but soon you will begin to know what is from your flesh and what is from your spirit. The person prayed over will exclaim, "How did you know? As soon as you said 'Anger' something in me just bubbled up."

The Ways of Demons

Discernment through a knowing often merges with pure knowledge of the ways of demons, and it takes very little else to know what follows. For instance, the moment you hear the person start to scream or wail, you may recognize a Witchcraft spirit. Witchcraft usually comes out with high pitched screams and body tenseness. It doesn't matter if the spirit is Kahuna, Gypsy, Witchcraft, Buddhist, Jezebel, Virgin Mary, or any other form of witchcraft and occult. When exposed, that spirit wails or screams.

If the person starts to clutch her neck and shoulders, consider Rejection and Pride. Jezebel loves to hide in the joints and the marrow of the bone, especially of the spine. Pride often brings pain to the heart or the lower back. If the person starts having a headache, most likely occult Mind Control will manifest.

Knowledge of different spirits and how they operate also aids in discernment. As I attempt to impart some insights as to different spirits and deliverance techniques, we need to keep in mind that we don't know everything, need to pay attention to the Holy Spirit, and must not limit Him. Always seek diligently the Holy Spirit's guidance. Don't bottle Him up; instead, let Him work through you.

Increased knowledge of the spiritual realm includes a deeper understanding of Satan's spiritual kingdom, how he operates, the major spirits he uses, their names and characteristics, and how they work in these end times. What are their strengths and weaknesses? What are their tactics and ways of operating? How does God reveal their identities in the Word? How does God show us the weapons of our spirit and how to apply them? Often, knowledge supplements discernment. Once the Holy Spirit reveals a particular spirit, past knowledge brings to mind everything known about this demon. Practice sharpens your spirit, so don't run away from a battle.

Sharing knowledge about the satanic kingdom does not glorify Satan. It helps defeat him. Nothing in this book glorifies Satan. It exposes his vulnerability to the Word of God and the blood of the Lamb.

As you continue in spiritual warfare, your discernment will grow more acute. Just trust God; He knows your heart and will outfit you with the necessary discernment. If you desire to learn deliverance, God will meet you with all the tools necessary, provided you walk in obedience to the Holy Spirit. Praise God!

Chapter Six

Binding and Loosing

In an earlier chapter, I mentioned that Satan rules from the mid-heavens over a well organized army. He divides the earth into principalities ruled over by princes, also called strongmen. The strongmen sit on thrones in the mid-heavens and rule over the evil spirits on earth. They give orders and strength to the spirits under their command. Other strongmen operate on the earth itself. I believe there are actually three levels of strongmen: (1) rulers over principalities or wide geographic areas on earth; (2) rulers over people, churches, families, communities, and other specific groups or individuals; and (3) rulers who dwell within people.

The Strongman Must Be Bound

Unless we bind up the strongmen, it is difficult to cast out demons. In Matthew 16:19, Jesus instructs us to bind up the strongman. He repeats his admonition in Mark 3:27 and warns us in Matthew 12:29 that we cannot spoil the strongman's house unless we first bind up the strongman: "*Or else how can one enter into a strong man's house, and spoil his goods, except he first bind the strongman? and then he will spoil his house.*"

It is a literal truism. Unless you bind the strongman, you will experience incredible difficulty in casting out the lesser demons. The lesser demons will continue to draw strength from the strongman or ruling spirit. It's as if there is a gas line between the strongman and the spirits under it. Bind the strongman and cut off its cords, and the spirits under the strongman weaken. All military strategists understand the necessity of cutting off the enemy's supply line.

The church badly needs to learn how to bind the enemy both here on earth and in the heavenlies. The fight is in the spirit realm, so we act by faith in the Word of God. We cannot see the strongman, but we know its works.

> *For we wrestle not against flesh and blood, but against principalities, against powers, against the rulers of the darkness of this world, against spiritual wickedness in high places.* (Eph. 6:12)

"*Rulers of the darkness of this world*" and "*spiritual wickedness in high places*" refer to strongmen.

Our Authority

The authority to bind up the strongman comes from our Lord Jesus Himself.

*And I give unto thee the keys of the kingdom
of heaven: and whatsoever thou shalt bind on
earth shall be bound in heaven: and whatsoever thou shalt loose on earth shall be loosed
in heaven.* (Matt. 16:19)

Again, in Matthew 18:18, He says:

*Verily I say unto you, Whatsoever ye shall
bind on earth shall be bound in heaven: and
whatsoever ye shall loose on earth shall be
loosed in heaven.*

Satan devises a plan for every one of us. Several
Christians claim that God actually showed them Satan's war room where he drafts schemes to destroy
every marriage, relationship, and church. What plan
does Satan have for you? What strongman rules
over your church? If you know the strongman, you
know his plans. To know the strongman, look to the
fruits. Jesus said, *"Ye shall know them by their
fruits"* (Matt. 7:16).

People reject the Gospel of peace because the
god of this world blinds them, not necessarily because they consciously reject the Word:

*In whom the god of this world hath blinded
the minds of them which believe not, lest the
light of the glorious gospel of Christ, who is
the image of God, should shine unto them.*
(2 Cor. 4:4)

Bind up the strongman who blinds them, and
they will accept the Gospel, or at least come to a decision without outside interference.

In one episode, the pastor of our church took every opportunity to lead Howard (not his real name) to the Lord. Each time, Howard shook his head and declared that he was not ready. Finally one night, the pastor engaged Howard in conversation on some trivial subject. While Howard spoke on the subject, I sat on the side binding up the blinding spirits and commanded them to release Howard's spiritual eyes. After about ten minutes, Howard paused in his conversation and the pastor said, "By the way, Howard, are you ready to receive Jesus Christ in your life tonight?" Howard looked at the pastor, smiled, and said, "Why not? I'm ready." Howard became one more for the kingdom, and his family wept with joy as he received Jesus into his life. Dr. Rebecca Brown, in her book, *Prepare for War*, brings this out magnificently.

Offensive or Defensive?

Office turmoil, bickering among family members or fellow workers, depression, failures in life—these smack of demonic oppression. My daughter came home crying almost every day about her work and the people in her office. The very day she started binding up the spirits of discord in the office, she stopped complaining. It was demonic.

You need to get on the offensive. Gird up your armor and run to the battle. How do you bind up the strongman? In faith, simply say:

I bind up the ruling spirit of _____ in the heavenlies with chains from heaven. I stand on the Word of God that says,

> *And I will give unto thee the keys of the king-*
> *dom of heaven: and whatsoever thou shalt*
> *bind on earth shall be bound in heaven: and*
> *whatsoever thou shalt loose on earth shall be*
> *loosed in heaven.* (Matt. 16:19)

I bind you up hand and foot, and I cut of all
cords between the ruling spirit and the spirits
in this person, and I cast them off in Jesus'
name.

Some discernment is required in order to know
which ruling spirit is the strongman. Although the
seven major ruling spirits control the principalities,
the actual strongman over a particular area or person may be not be one of the seven. For instance,
Witchcraft (occult), Rejection, Rebellion, Schizophrenia, Fear, Infirmity, Hate, Unforgiveness, and
the like can also act as ruling spirits.

Remember that ruling spirits also dwell in the
person. A specific ruling spirit rules over each nest or
stronghold. Some ruling spirits are obvious. For instance, in the area of witchcraft, Jezebel and Hades
rule. In terminal illnesses, Death and Infirmity rule.

Hierarchies Within

Spirits sometimes have a hierarchy which they
refuse to violate. In one case, a spirit of Lung Cancer refused to leave. Upon questioning, the spirit
said he couldn't leave because High Blood Pressure
blocked him. Unless High Blood Pressure left first,

he couldn't. When we cast out High Blood Pressure, Lung Cancer left. Of course, spirits could be trying to fool you by stalling for time. The same thing, however, occurred a number of times and gave rise to my conclusion that a hierarchy among demons can exist.

Jezebel rules like a queen. She has many servants and lesser spirits that serve her. To get to her, you may need to go after the many lesser spirits first. She simply retreats to the innermost chamber and sits on the throne while the spirits under her try to confuse and stop you. Jezebel will toss up many spirits such as Rejection, Anger, Unforgiveness, Rebellion, Jealousy, Hatred, Murder, and Violence before she can be reached. These spirits will simply manifest in the person. It reminds me of invading a castle and meeting many foot soldiers blocking the path while the queen retreats to the innermost chamber hidden in the darkest recesses of the castle where she is attended by her many servants and handmaidens. Like Leviathan, you will not soon forget a fight with Jezebel. In order to defeat her, the person being delivered must have an intense desire to persevere until victory is gained.

It Does Not Last Forever

The Bible does not indicate that a ruling spirit bound in the heavenlies remains bound forever. Just as we need to put on our armor of God daily, we also need to bind up the strongmen periodically, if not daily. As mentioned earlier, Pastor Yonggi Cho of South Korea attributes his success in South

Korea to binding up of the strongman. It took one year of constant prayer—24 hours a day, 365 days a year to bind up the strongman over that country. People prayed all night as a body at least once a week, and individuals volunteered to pray so that prayers went up to the throne of God around the clock. Today, people in South Korea pray twenty-four hours a day to keep the strongman bound.

We need to make a distinction between strongmen in the heavenlies assigned to a particular person and those who control a particular principality. The strongman over a person can be bound by workers without too much problem; however, the ruling prince over a wide area represents a more formidable adversary and requires corporate prayers.

Warring in the Heavens

If God's people intend to take this earth for the kingdom of God, they must first take the heavenlies. The strongman over each area must be bound in order to release the souls of men, women, and children. As mentioned above, when asked the reason for his success, Pastor Yonggi (Paul) Cho, founder of the world's largest church (400,000 members at last count), said very succinctly, "We bound up the strongman over Korea."

The strongman over principalities controls many people, and his jurisdiction extends over a wide geographic area, as compared to a strongman over a single person or over a neighborhood. The strongman will not bend to just a few saints. God has designated His true church, the body of Christ, to defeat principalities (Jer. 51:20–21). The gates of hell shall not prevail against the church. It is the church that is designated by God to tear down hell's gates. No individual saint fights that battle alone. It takes the united effort of God's people to bind up the strongman over different areas. One of the jobs of God's end-time army is to war in the heavenlies against Satan's high command and Satan himself.

In order to accomplish the task of dealing with principalities, the body of Christ must come together in unity of spirit and prayer. We are not talking about loose, disconnected, or occasional prayer. It will require a concerted effort by the body of Christ, praying continuously.

> *Behold, how good and how pleasant it is for brethren to dwell together in unity! It is like the precious ointment upon the head, that ran down upon the beard, even Aaron's beard: that went down to the skirts of his garments; as the dew of Hermon, and as the dew that descended upon the mountains of Zion: for there the LORD commanded the blessing, even life forevermore.* (Ps. 133:1–3)

There is tremendous strength in unity. Satan knows this and that is why he tries his best to keep the body of Christ divided. The precious ointment is the oil of anointing that God promises. Unity brings an anointing upon the church that Satan cannot stand against.

In the Middle East, it is usually hot and dry during the day. However, it cools at night so in the morning there is dew on the plants. Without this dew, the plants would perish. When the people of Israel lived in the wilderness with Moses, the dew that evaporated in the morning left manna that fed the people and gave them life. Hermon and Zion are synonymous words. Where there is unity, God will command the blessing, even life forevermore. God's true church in the end times will move in a unity the world has never before seen.

Even today, God is raising up a body of prayer and deliverance warriors that will come together one day to form the great army of God. I do not have all the answers, but I can share what I do know and trust that God will reveal the rest later.

In several prophecies over our local church, God declared that He will have believers used as arrows of lighting in the sky to knock off principalities. In a recent men's retreat, the men stood in unity and rose up against the strongmen over the retreat. As they prayed and conducted unified spiritual warfare, God gave several men visions of rows of angels battling in the heavenlies for the church. Bolts of lightning came from the men who were praying in unison, binding up principalities. These bolts began tearing large holes in the brazen skies. The strongmen were startled.

The Bible talks about God's lightning arrows (2 Sam 22:15; Ps. 144:6). The combined prayers of the saints will be like arrows of lightning shooting down principalities. For this reason, the local churches are being called back into prayer and intercession.

Chapter Seven

The Blood of Jesus

A nd they overcame him [Satan] *by the blood of the Lamb*" (Rev. 12:11). If Christians come to an understanding of how precious and powerful the blood of our Savior is in our walk, they would be well on the way to being overcomers. The precious blood of our Lord not only serves as an atonement for our sins, it totally devastates the demonic realm. At mention of the blood of Jesus, demons literally tremble with fear. They may remain silent for a few moments, but they will soon cry out, "Stop it!" The blood cleanses in the spirit, and burns the demons. The powers of darkness can never stand against the blood of Jesus Christ.

Like most things in the spirit, faith must be an active ingredient in claiming the blood or using it as a weapon. Faith comes through hearing, and hearing by the Word of God. There are many good books about the blood of Jesus, including H. Maxwell Whyte's *The Power of the Blood*, *The Overcoming Blood* by Bob Lamb, and Dr. M. R. DeHaan's *The Chemistry of the Blood*.

The blood is precious to man because it is precious to God. God shows us very early in the Word the importance of blood to Him and all mankind. Genesis 3:21 says, "*Unto Adam also and to his wife did the LORD God make coats of skins, and clothed them.*" To obtain skins, blood had to be shed. Adam and Eve covered themselves with fig leaves, but fig leaves will never do. Only blood can provide a covering for mankind. The word "atonement" means "covering." Only blood will cover our sins. God already had plans to save mankind. He knew the precious blood of his Son would one day be shed for the world.

In Genesis chapter four, God respected Abel's sacrifice of a lamb, but He rejected Cain's sacrifice of fruits and vegetables. God showed that a sacrifice through blood was the only sacrifice acceptable to Him. Cain misunderstood, and many Christians also misunderstand the importance of the blood. Fig-leaf coverings and vegetable sacrifices will never do. Churches that do not know the power of the blood of Jesus have fig-leaf and vegetable ministries. Cain doubtlessly worked hard for his fruits and vegetables; but no matter how hard he worked, no matter how many fruits and vegetables he grew and gathered, it could not provide a covering for sin. In church terms, no matter how many good works a person does, if the Lamb's blood is not in his life, there is no salvation, no atonement, and no pleasing God.

It Turns Away Death

When Moses led the people of God out of Egypt, God again demonstrated the power of the blood.

This time, God showed us that the blood turns away even death. In Exodus 12:7 and 13, God instructed Moses to have the people kill a perfect lamb, one for each household of fifteen people, and to sprinkle its blood on the sideposts and lintel of the door. When the Angel of Death passed by, it did not enter any household with the blood so sprinkled, for God did not allow it to enter. Death is an enemy. The Bible says that Jesus will sit at the right hand of the Father until all of His enemies are put under his feet. *"For he must reign, till he hath put all enemies under his feet. The last enemy that shall be destroyed is death"* (1 Cor. 15:25–26).

Life defeats death. The Bible says that the life is in the blood—not the heart, kidneys, or brains (Lev. 17:11, 14). The life of Jesus is in His blood. It is the life in the blood that turns back death.

Only God's perfect Passover Lamb, Jesus Christ, will do. It is His blood that protects us from death and gives us everlasting life. His blood compels death to pass over. No fig leaves or fruits will do it—no good works—just faith, the grace of God, and the blood of the Lamb.

It Atones

It is the blood that atones for the soul.

For the life of the flesh is in the blood: and I have given it to you upon the altar to make an atonement for your souls: for it is the blood that maketh an atonement for the soul.

.(Lev. 17:11)

131

That is why God so strongly admonished the people against eating or drinking blood. Blood is precious. One cannot disrespect it or look upon it in a trivial manner. God will not allow it because one day, His beloved Son would shed His blood for mankind and wash away the veil between the Father and us.

The blood atones or covers sin. Hebrews 9:22 says, *"Without shedding of blood is no remission* [of sins]." Without His shed blood, we would be forever doomed.

It Saves

God took careful steps to teach us about the saving power of the blood. Rahab, the harlot who along with her family was saved from destruction, was instructed to tie a scarlet thread on her window. When Jericho's walls fell, only Rahab's house was spared. No lamb was available, so the spies used a scarlet thread. That scarlet thread represented blood. It saved Rahab and her entire family.

It was the crucifixion of Jesus Christ the Son of God that tore the veil between God and man and brought reconciliation (Rom. 5:10; 2 Cor. 5:18). Now, we call Him Abba Father, and He calls us sons and daughters. The blood made it possible for the prodigal sons to come home. It saves!

It Heals

In the Old Testament, the prescribed way to cleanse a leper was to place the blood of a lamb on his right ear, thumb, and big toe. The blood cleansed the people of all types of diseases. To those in the flesh, it had to be one of the strangest ways to heal sickness, but to God it was the only way. It was a type and shadow for those of us today who believe in Jesus Christ.

It is the blood that heals, and it continues to do so today. It comes from the Son who sits at the right hand of the Father. The Bible promises that we are healed by His stripes (Isa. 53:5; 1 Pet. 2:24). Thirty-nine stripes slashed His back, and the cruel whip with a piece of bone at the end tore His flesh and ripped it apart. Under Roman law, a man could not be whipped more than forty times, and if the person administering the whipping exceeded that amount, he would in turn be punished severely. Therefore, to make sure that forty strips was not exceeded accidentally, they stopped at thirty-nine.

Medical books separate all types of disease and sickness into thirty-nine categories. It is no coincidence that the number of stripes on His back was thirty-nine. It's the blood from the stripes that heals. Jesus sits in glory at the right hand of the Father, but His blood still heals on earth. Its power can never be lost.

It Consecrates

The priests in Moses' day were ordained by placing blood on their right ears, hands, and feet. The blood cleansed them of sin and set them apart for service unto God. God designated the tribe of Levi for priestly duties. Not all Levites were priests, but all priests were Levites. Those called to service in the temple were consecrated by the blood. Jesus Christ, the Son of God, sits at the right hand of the Father. He consecrated Himself for service unto the Father and all of mankind. It is His blood that consecrates and sets aside those who desire to serve through the blood.

It Was Poured on the Earth

Many times in the Old Testament, God demonstrated the importance of blood. The priests in Moses' tabernacle poured out the blood of the animal sacrifices onto the ground around the brazen altar at the entrance to the tabernacle, just inside the gate. If you draw a line from the brazen altar to the ark of the covenant and then from the candlestick to the table of showbread, it forms a perfect cross. The brazen altar represents the foot of the cross. The blood of the sacrifice was poured unto the ground there. The priests sprinkled some of the blood on various items of furniture in the Holy Place, and on the mercy seat in the Holy of Holies, but they poured most of the blood out on the ground around the brazen altar.

One day, much blood would be poured out on the earth at the foot of the cross on Calvary. There was blood on the cross, on His hands, feet, back, and head. The blood poured down His arms, sides, and legs down into the earth.

He was from heaven and came to shed His blood for those on earth. He hung between heaven and earth. He was God, and yet He was fully man. He is called the Son of God, and yet He is also called the Son of Man, even in heaven (Rev. 14:14). He came to create a new race of people who dwell on earth but who are citizens of heaven. Jesus is the firstborn of the dead (Col. 1:18). He is the Alpha and Omega, the beginning and the end (Rev 1:8, 11; 21:6; 22:13). There is no other like Him. His blood is poured out on the earth, but it never dies, it never dries up, it never rots, it never becomes corrupted. It lives forever. It is on the earth for all those who believe.

There's So Much Blood

If you consider how many animals Israel slaughtered as sin sacrifices from Moses' day until the coming of Jesus, it will astonish you. For instance, most Bible scholars claim that between two million and three and one-half million Israelites took part in the exodus from Egypt. Fifteen people comprised one household. If so, then the Hebrew people killed between 133,333 and 233,333 lambs on the first Passover day. In Solomon's day, Bible scholars estimate that over 6,000,000 Israelites lived in Israel. That means at least 400,000 animals shed their blood when Solomon's temple was dedicated. The blood would have flowed like a river. Even if those figures are exaggerated, the blood would have been like a river. Can you imagine how many animals shed blood between the time of Moses and Jesus' crucifixion?

You see, God wants us to know that the blood of Jesus covers the earth. It flows like a river, never drying up, never ending. There's blood enough for all. Historians report that the Wales Revival of the early 1900's began when God gave a preacher's wife a vision of the blood of Jesus flowing and pouring upon the earth like Niagara Falls. "There's so much blood," she cried out. Whenever God's people called out, "The blood of Jesus," the Holy Spirit fell on the meeting, and the revival began. Thereafter, the call of "The blood of Jesus" and "There's power in the blood" became the rallying cry for Christians everywhere. There is no substitute for the blood; it still cries out.

It Washes Clean

In Moses' day, God had His priests put on white linen garments (Lev. 6:10). God was showing mankind heavenly things. Before Jesus walked the earth in flesh, God had to give those who appeared in His heavenly presence holy garments (Zech. 3:5). Isaiah 61:10 says,

> *I will greatly rejoice in the LORD, my soul shall be joyful in my God; for he hath clothed me with the garments of salvation, he hath covered me with the robe of righteousness.*

After Jesus Christ shed His precious blood for the world, the garments of righteousness could be obtained only through a washing by His blood. Animal sacrifice was no longer acceptable to God. In Revelation 6:11, the Scriptures talk about the martyrs in heaven: "*And white robes were given unto every one of them.*" Revelation 7:9 says, "*a great multitude...stood before the throne, and before the Lamb,*

clothed with white robes, and palms in their hands."
Who these saints are and how their robes became
white is explained in Revelation 7:14: "*These are they
which came out of great tribulation, and have washed
their robes, and made them white in the blood of the
Lamb*." There can be no garments of righteousness
without washing by His precious blood. Jesus said,

> *I counsel thee to buy of me gold tried in the
> fire, that thou mayest be rich; and white rai-
> ment, that thou mayest be clothed, and that
> the shame of thy nakedness do not appear.*
> (Rev. 3:18)

His blood covers our sins. When God looks upon
us, He does not see our sins. He sees only white
garments cleansed by the blood.

There's Blood in Heaven

There is enough blood of Jesus to burn every
demon in Satan's kingdom and to save every sinner.
There's blood in heaven too. In Revelation 5:6, Jesus,
the Lamb of God, stands before the throne, as if slain.
There is blood on the Lamb. When the Father sees
the blood on the Lamb, He knows that Jesus shed
His precious blood for you and me. The Father sees
only the blood of His Son. Praise God! The blood
covers (atones for) us. He accepts us without reserve.
We can now come boldly into the very throne room
of God because of the blood (Heb. 10:19).

The blood covers all believers. The blood atones
for our sins and covers us. The blood makes us

kings and priests unto God. As God's priests, we minister in the Holy Place and even the Holy of Holies before the throne of God. There is blood not only in heaven, in the Holy of Holies, but also on earth where the body of Christ ministers to Him. The body should minister to both believers and all sinners.

The Blood, Word, and Spirit Agree

Pleading the blood brings the Holy Spirit like nothing else. You see, the Spirit, water, and blood agree on earth. Water often stands for the Word of God. Ephesians 5:26 says, *"That he might...cleanse it* [the church] *with washing of water by the word."*
Blood sanctifies the Word.

> *For when Moses had spoken every precept to all the people according to the law, he took the blood of calves and of goats, with water, and scarlet wool, and hyssop, and sprinkled both the book, and all the people.* (Heb. 9:19)

Without the Cross and the blood, the Word alone would not bring salvation.

The Word, therefore, agrees with the blood. The Holy Spirit agrees with the blood. He comes quickly when you claim the blood of Jesus with faith. First John 5:8 says, *"And there are three that bear witness in earth, the Spirit, and the water, and the blood: and these three agree in one."*

Mention the blood or the Word, and the Holy Spirit agrees. Plead the blood or confess the Word, and the Spirit responds. God not only inhabits the praises of His people, He responds to the blood and the Word. The Word and the blood agree because it is the blood that empowers the Word and the Word that confesses the blood.

In Summary

Pleading the blood of Jesus in a deliverance session usually brings immediate results. Claim the power of the blood, and ask Jesus to cover the person with His precious blood. Dry up all waters of the enemy.

The Bible doesn't exactly prescribe the way the blood is to be used to cast out demons, neither does the Bible outline how to break curses, but I do believe that the saints, acting as kings and priests of God, have been given charge over the blood.

The overcomers in Revelation 12:11 overcome Satan with the blood of the Lamb, the word of their testimonies, and their love which is greater for God than for their earthly lives. The blood of the Lamb is a powerful weapon for all Christians! Praise Jesus for His precious blood!

Chapter Eight

Drying Up the Enemy's Waters

Two kinds of waters exist side by side—the waters of God and the waters of Satan. One gives life, the other death. The Bible often describes the Holy Spirit as rivers of living water. The Bible also alludes to the Word of God as water. Ephesians 5:26 says, *"the washing of water by the word."* The Word cleanses and renews like water. Jesus talked to the woman at the well about living waters:

> But whosoever drinketh of the water that I
> shall give him shall never thirst; but the water
> that I shall give him shall be in him a well of
> water springing up into everlasting life.
>
> (John 4:14)

Jesus spoke to the Samaritan woman about the waters of life. In John 7:38, Jesus said, *"He that believeth on me, as the scripture hath said, out of his belly shall flow rivers of living water."* In Revelation

140

21:6, the Lord said, "*I will give unto him that is athirst of the fountain of the water of life freely.*" God's waters bring life everlasting.

River of Death

Satan, of course, loves to counterfeit everything God does. He also counterfeits the waters of life with his waters of death.

In Greek and Roman mythology, the River Styx represents the river of death. The boatman, Charon, takes departed souls across the river and drops them off on the other side to the kingdom of Hades.

Orientals also believe in a river that must be crossed to get to paradise or the nether world. Taoists burn paper clothes and money at funerals. According to Chinese legend, without money to pay the river boatman, your spirit cannot get over to the other side and could end up wandering this earth.

Writers often call the River Jordan a river of death. To get to the promised land, all men must first cross the waters of death. You may recall that Joshua and the entire Hebrew nation crossed over on dry ground to reach the promised land. The priests carried the ark of the covenant as all Israel looked steadfastly at the ark, a type of Jesus.

> *And it shall come to pass, as soon as the soles of the feet of the priests that bear the ark of the LORD, the Lord of all the earth, shall rest in the waters of Jordan, that the waters of Jordan shall be cut off from the waters that come down from above; and they shall stand upon an heap....all the Israelites passed over on dry*

141

*ground, until all the people were passed clean
over Jordan.* (Josh. 3:13, 17)

Death Defeated

So it will be in the end times when some of the
people of God shall pass over into the promised land
on dry ground. Jesus Christ, the ark of God's testimony, shall lead the way. As their feet touch the
waters of the River of Death, the waters shall fall
back. Death shall be put under their feet and destroyed (1 Cor. 15:25–26).

Elijah is a forerunner to the sons of God in the
end times. In 2 Kings 2:8, Elijah and Elisha walked
together just before Elijah was taken to heaven. *"And
Elijah took his mantle, and wrapped it together, and
smote the waters, and they were divided hither and
thither, so that they two went over on dry land."*
Soon thereafter, Elijah went to heaven without
tasting death. God has authority over the waters
(Ps. 78:13), and so do the people of God.

Since the wages of sin is death (Rom. 6:23), one
cannot separate the waters of death from sin. The
waters of death work in each sinner and give demonic forces strength and the right to operate in his
life. The waters of death give strength to evil spirits.
Small wonder that God promises to dry up the waters of the enemy in the end times.

Drying Up the Waters

Jeremiah 50:38 says, *"A drought is upon her
waters; and they shall be dried up: for it is the land*

of graven images, and they are mad upon their idols." In Jeremiah 51:36, the Bible says, "*Therefore thus saith the LORD; Behold, I will plead thy cause, and take vengeance for thee; and I will dry up her sea, and make her springs dry.*" The prophet is talking about Babylon the great, the ugly and powerful spirit that reigns in the end times. Her sea infers a spiritual medium of sin and evil that draws multitudes of people into captivity. Millions are drowning in the waters of sin and death. The Word says:

> *The burden of Tyre. Howl, ye ships of Tarshish; for it is laid waste, so that there is no house, no entering in: from the land of Chittim it is revealed to them. Be still, ye inhabitants of the isle; thou whom the merchants of Zidon, that pass over the sea, have replenished. And by great waters the seed of Sihor, the harvest of the river, is her revenue; and she is a mart of nations. Be thou ashamed, O Zidon: for the sea hath spoken, even the strength of the sea, saying, I travail not, nor bring forth children, neither do I nourish up young men, nor bring up virgins.*
>
> (Isa. 23:1–4)

The words "Tyre," "Tarshish," and "Zidon," refer to Babylon the great, the Queen of Babylon. Zidon draws strength from the waters of sin and death.

There are prophecies about the demise of Egypt (which is synonymous with Babylon):

> *And the waters shall fail from the sea, and the river shall be wasted and dried up. And they*

*shall turn the rivers far away; and the brooks
of defence shall be emptied and dried up: the
reeds and flags shall wither.* (Isa. 19:5–6)

In Revelation 17:3, this ugly spirit called Mystery, Babylon the Great, Mother of Harlots, and Abominations of the Earth, sits on a beast that appears to be the same beast that arises from the sea in Revelation 13:1.

Waters or seas are also related to Leviathan, the spirit of Pride, who is a dragon of the sea. The psalmist says:

*Thou didst divide the sea by thy strength:
thou brakest the heads of the dragons in the
waters. Thou brakest the heads of Leviathan
in pieces, and gavest him to be meat to the
people inhabiting the wilderness.*

(Ps. 74:13–14)

It is no small wonder that Pride dwells in the waters of death. Pride leads to sin and sin to death. From top to bottom, every demon in hell is full of pride. Psalm 124:4–5 says, *"Then the waters had overwhelmed us, the stream had gone over our soul. Then the proud waters had gone over our soul."* The psalmist describes the waters as "proud" waters. They are the deadly waters of Pride.

Waters also represent death and disaster. Psalm 18:16 says, *"he drew me out of many waters."* Psalm 69:1–2 says, *"Save me, O God; for the waters are come in unto my soul. I sink in deep mire, where there is no standing: I am come into deep waters, where the floods overflow me."* Psalm 144:7 says, *"Send thine hand from above; rid me, and deliver me out of great waters, from the hand of strange children."*

God promises to dry up the waters of the enemy in many Scriptures. Obviously, drying up the waters of the enemy weakens them and brings defeat to the demonic kingdom. Nahum 1:4 says, *"He rebuketh the sea, and maketh it dry, and drieth up all the rivers."* In Isaiah 19:5, the prophet talks about the fall of Egypt:

> *And the waters shall fail from the sea, and the river shall be wasted and dried up. And they shall turn the rivers far away; and the brooks of defence shall be emptied and dried up: the reeds and flags shall wither.*

Egypt was an enemy of God. She stood where Babylon once stood. She drew strength from her rivers. Dry up her waters, and she loses her power. To the Hebrew people, Egypt represented the world and death.

In Isaiah 44, the prophet commands Israel to rejoice because the Lord has redeemed them, *"that sayeth to the deep, Be dry, and I will dry up thy rivers"* (v. 27). There is a definite link between the destruction of Babylon (Egypt) and her waters. As deliverers, we need to understand the role and importance of drying up her waters.

We could go on and on in exploring the waters of death and their use by Satan and his hordes. The point is that evil spirits move in a type of evil, spiritual "water," but God promises to dry up the seas so that they will no longer draw strength from the waters.

Deliverance Techniques

During a deliverance session, I find it very powerful to declare to the enemy the following:

> In the name of Jesus, I dry up your waters, your seas, your rivers, and your springs. I stand on the Word of God, and I cause a drought over your land. Pass over to Chittim; you shall find no rest. There is no water; there's only the blood of Jesus. I make your habitation a desolate wilderness.

During deliverance, drying up the waters of the enemy represents a major weapon in the hands of God's people. In many cases, the person being prayed over will suddenly start to act as if his throat has become parched. He will swallow and smack his mouth looking for water. The demons will start to weaken and may scream obscenities. When that happens, you know that they are unable to draw strength from the waters of death, and their defeat is imminent.

In Matthew 12:43, Jesus says, "*When the unclean spirit is gone out of a man, he walketh through dry places, seeking rest, and findeth none.*" Demons hate dry places. They cannot find strength or rest there. They find no evil waters of death to strengthen them. In a deliverance session, it may also be helpful to remind them that they must go to the dry places as written in God's Word (Matt. 12:43; Luke 11:24).

Chapter Nine

The Gates

The strength or vulnerability of an ancient walled city rested in its gates. Some strongholds featured only one gate. Others contained more than one. In times of danger from invasion, the people living in the countryside and adjoining areas fled to the protection of walled fortresses or cities. Jericho, in the book of Joshua, was such a city.

These strongholds or fortresses were usually surrounded by thick walls, a drawbridge, and high, thick gates made of strong bars of brass or iron (2 Chron. 14:7). If the enemy took the gates, they won the battle. Even in peacetime, gates held important significance. The elders of the city took their positions at the gate and observed everyone passing through the gates. They stopped suspicious travelers and took record of each one who passed through. Often, the city builders constructed the meeting place for the governing body of the city next to the gates or even above the gates. At each entrance, the city elders posted armed sentries to guard the gate. Whoever controlled the gates ruled the city.

Obviously, the city fathers made the gates as strong as possible. The enemies, coming from outside, often sought to break the gates down by smashing it with battering rams and fire. Of course, they paid a high price for any attempt, since the design of the towers or the walls above the gate allowed archers to shower arrows down upon intruders at the gates. Hot burning tar also poured down, and sometimes huge rocks dropped from the gates' high towers.

Hell also contains gates. Jesus says that the gates of hell shall not prevail against the church (Matt. 16:18). Every believer should know this.

The Gatekeeper

I liken enemy strongholds in a person's body, soul, and spirit to ancient cities with high walls, thick gates, and moats. In the spirit realm, there are gates or entrances to a person's body and soul which the enemy attacks. Once a gate is conquered, the ruling spirit appoints a powerful demon to act as gatekeeper. The gatekeeper controls the gate from that point on. He opens it up to allow other demons to enter. For instance, if a person allows Sexual Lust to rule, the spirit will soon invite Adultery, Fornication, Perversion, Homosexuality, Uncleanness, Masturbation, and other sexually related spirits to enter. He closes and defends the gates during attacks from Christians. Unless you bind up the gatekeeper, expect some heavy fighting at the gates during a deliverance session. The gatekeeper is usually the ruling spirit.

Walls of Babylon

Archeologists claim that the city of Babylon surrounded itself with the strongest and most fortified double walls ever constructed by man. Two thick walls surrounded the entire city. The walls were so thick that chariots raced on the top of the walls between two rows of dwellings. They sometimes contained dwellings within its width as well— as with Rahab in the book of Joshua. The River Euphrates wound under the outer wall and between the two walls of Babylon. If one somehow got past the deep river in front and under the first wall, he found himself confronted by an impenetrable thick and strong two-leaved gate. Historians considered Babylon impregnable. God thought otherwise.

> *Thus saith the LORD to his anointed, to Cyrus, whose right hand I have holden, to subdue nations before him; and I will loose the loins of kings, to open before him the two leaved gates; and the gates shall not be shut; I will go before thee, and make the crooked places straight: I will break in pieces the gates of brass, and cut in sunder the bars of iron.*
>
> (Isa. 45:1–2)

Miraculously, when the armies of Cyrus approached the huge double-doored gates that protected the city, the gates lay in shatters, torn to pieces. God had torn them down. They entered the city unopposed and the slaughter commenced. After the battle, Cyrus saw the Scriptures, and he knew instantly that the victory was from God. He immediately sought to fulfill God's will by freeing the Israelites and supporting their attempts to return to their homeland to rebuild the holy city.

God Will Tear Down the Enemy's Gates

God promises to break the gates of the enemy for His people.

> *Oh, that men would praise the LORD for his goodness, and for his wonderful works to the children of men! For he hath broken the gates of brass, and cut the bars of iron asunder.*
>
> (Ps. 107:15–16)

Jesus Christ Himself holds the keys to hell and death. In Revelation 1:18, Jesus says, *"I am he that liveth, and was dead; and, behold, I am alive for evermore, Amen; and have the keys of hell and death."* Keys, of course, presuppose doors or gates.

As prophesied in Isaiah 22:22, the power of the key of David is shown in Revelation 3:7: *"These things saith he that is holy, he that is true, he that hath the key of David, he that openeth, and no man shutteth; and shutteth, and no man openeth."*

The gates of the enemy in the end times shall be taken by God's people. Nahum 2:6 says, *"The gates of the rivers shall be opened, and the palace shall be dissolved."* Deliverance workers well know how Jezebel (Babylon the Great) builds palaces or strongholds and hides therein.

God commands us to destroy the strongholds of Satan. In Isaiah 23:11, the prophet says,

> *He stretched out his hand over the sea, he shook the kingdoms: the LORD hath given a commandment against the merchant city, to destroy the strong holds thereof.*

That prophecy is for today also.

Techniques for Deliverance

In deliverance, we need to bind the gatekeeper, tear down the gates of the enemy, and knock down the pillars and the walls. When going after Jezebel, the gates represent a formidable barrier. The heathens called this ugly spirit the Goddess of Fortresses and Walled Cities (she was originally named Semiramis) and the Goddess of Warfare. The Bible describes her as a clever and devious enemy. She flees to the innermost parts of her stronghold and hides. She also throws up many lesser spirits in order to confuse the deliverance workers. You need to keep after her until you reach her inner throne room. You will find her there in all her nakedness and ugliness. She dwells deep in the hearts of men and women.

I often use the following sequence of commands in deliverance:

> I bind up the gatekeeper in the name of Jesus. He who has the key of David, what gate

or door he opens, none shall close, and what gate He closes, none shall open. In the name of Jesus, and by the authority given me by Jesus, I tear down your two-leaved gates, I knock down your pillars, I smash down your walls. No stone shall stand upon another. (Rev. 3:7; Isa. 22:22; Ezek. 21:15–22).

Our Own Gates

We have gates to our spirits, souls, and bodies. Thank God the Holy Spirit seals our spirit. But we can still be oppressed in the spirit. God warns us to protect our own gates with righteousness, peace, and truth (Zech. 8:16; Ps. 118:19). As a person is delivered, you need to shut all open gates against the enemy. If even one gate is open, demons will try to slip in. Gates of Pride, Bitterness, Hatred, Unforgiveness, et cetera must be closed. Following repentance, simply ask Jesus to close each gate specifically so that no one shall open them. Prolonged sin will open gates to the soul and body. Another word for gates is "doors," and the Bible says this about doors:

> Then Moses called for all the elders of Israel, and said unto them, Draw out and take you a lamb according to your families, and kill the passover. And ye shall take a bunch of hyssop, and dip it in the blood that is in the basin, and strike the lintel and the two side posts with the blood that is in the basin; and none of you shall go out at the door of his house until the morning. For the LORD will pass

*through to smite the Egyptians; and when he
seeth the blood upon the lintel, and on the two
side posts, the LORD will pass over the door,
and will not suffer the destroyer to come in
unto your houses to smite you.*

(Exod. 12:21–23)

When we are not walking in righteousness, our
gates will be opened and our bars devoured by fire.
God warned the Israelites about the end times in
Nahum 3:13, *"Behold, thy people in the midst of thee
are women: the gates of thy land shall be set wide
open unto thine enemies: the fire shall devour thy
bars."*

We need to execute the judgment of truth and
peace in our gates (Zech. 8:16). Psalm 118:19 says,
*"Open to me the gates of righteousness: I will go into
them, and I will praise the LORD"* It is obvious that
our walk in the Lord, and His truth, peace, and
righteousness strengthen our gates against the enemy.

Chapter Ten

Preparing Yourself to Deliver

You need to consider at least four areas before entering into a deliverance session. First, prepare yourself; second, prepare the person to be delivered; third, prepare the deliverance team; fourth, prepare the physical location.

The Holy Spirit's Anointing

Deliverance usually doesn't happen without preparation unless the Holy Spirit summarily takes charge. When that happens, it takes place in a perfect setting with no harm to anyone. God simply is in control. For instance, a person may suddenly start screaming obscenities during a service. I can recall instances when strangers to the church started trembling as they walked through the front door. They coughed and choked for a few moments as demons fled. At a number of services, especially during the praise portion and sometimes during a sermon on deliverance, demons manifested in individuals who started screaming obscenities. In one case, the demons in a woman stood up and cried out, "Stop talking about me." She picked up a notebook and threw it at the pastor. The demon was immediately rebuked and came out. God is sovereign and anoints when and where He desires. He often acts without any preparation on the part of the deliverance worker. In normal situations, however, deliverance workers need to do certain things in order to prepare for the anointing.

I don't mean to imply that a formula exists whereby you can create anointing. You prepare for deliverance by your walk with God. As you abide in Him, the anointing continues (1 John 2:27; John 15:4–5, 7). Since every Christian should be able to cast out demons, the Christian walk itself should give you sufficient power or anointing to handle most deliverances. Certain situations, however, do require extra effort in the area of prayer and fasting. Jesus says that the Lunatic spirit comes out only by prayer and fasting (Matt. 17:21). Prayer and fasting increase faith, and supplications to God do not go unanswered.

Your Prayer Life

Christians should pray daily. Warfare prayers in the spirit set the stage for the casting out of some particularly troublesome spirit that resists ordinary deliverance. If the spirits in a person seem unusually strong, so much that some word of knowledge or wisdom is necessary, pray for the Holy Spirit's guidance. You need to know the will of God and how He wants you to proceed. There are other questions. What spirits control? How did they come in? What spirits need to be bound up? Are there still legal grounds for Satan to work? Prayer and the deliverance ministry go hand in hand. Often, the prayer session reveals hidden secrets and past events that the person has completely forgotten.

In one case, parents dedicated their baby daughter to Satan before she was born. In another, a relative put curses on the woman, and no one knew it. God revealed these things through prayer. Pray the victory before the fight. You simply don't barge into battle without praying the victory first, although sometimes God is merciful and deliverance succeeds in spite of the workers' unreadiness.

For the person just entering into a walk with God, daily prayer in the morning or at night brings many benefits. I have observed anointed deliverance ministers who do not appear to pray as much as I teach people to pray. However, these people are usually older Christians who have been evangelists and pastors for many years or have already established a solid relationship with God.

The apostle Paul admonishes us to pray always. Ephesians 6:18 says, *"praying always with all prayer."*

Fasting

As mentioned earlier, some demons can be handled only through fasting and prayer. As mentioned before, Jesus told His disciples that the

Lunatic spirit comes out only by fasting and prayer (Matt. 17:21; Mark 9:29). Many Christians shy away from fasting and prayer. If so, they deprive themselves of important weapons. Fasting aids spiritual growth. It helps you deny the flesh and the soul in order to make your spirit the master. Making the spirit master over the physical body and soul is absolutely necessary in any Christian's spiritual walk. The spirit should be under the total control of the Holy Spirit and needs to be kept in a cleansed condition for His use. People who fast often grow so used to fasting that the body and soul hardly resist anymore. Their pleadings and beggings simply don't work, and they give up.

The Old Testament shows that people knew about fasting: *"I humbled my soul with fasting"* (Psalm 35:13) and *"chastened my soul with fasting."* (Psalm 69:10). Daniel fasted (Dan. 9:3), as did the king (Dan 6:18). Joel 2:12, which talks about the end times, says, *"Therefore also now, saith the LORD, turn ye even to me with all your heart, and with fasting, and with weeping, and with mourning."*

"Oh, but that's Old Testament" you say. Sorry, the New Testament saints also fasted (Acts 10:30; Acts 14:23 for wisdom and blessings; Acts 27:33 for help; 1 Corinthians 7:5 to resist temptation).

Of course, if the Spirit does not lead you to fast, it becomes an unfruitful work. We need to ask God. If your conscience and intuition call you to fasting, obey it. On the other hand, make sure it's not your flesh. Those who dislike fasting will say, "The Holy Spirit told me I don't have to fast." Those who claim to be waiting for God to tell them when to fast almost never do. Don't shun fasting. Better to fast now and train the flesh than to pay the price later. Fasting serves as a mighty tool for giving the spirit rulership over your flesh and mind.

A Clean Heart of Love

Casting out demons, healing the sick, raising the dead and prophesying are manifestations of power in your walk, but it will never change your heart. Power can corrupt. Saul had power to destroy the enemies of God, accumulate great wealth, and become famous, but he was rebellious and self-centered until the end. Without love, all our works are worthless (1 Cor. 13:1–3).

Demons know when a Christian is rebellious and can attack because a door is open through sin. I experienced a case where one saint spoke against a leader publicly and was attacked by demons that very night. A person can fast, pray, and read the Word continuously, but if his heart is still prideful and has little love, the anointing of the Lord will be limited. When you are in the deliverance ministry, you need to keep your heart pure and filled with love.

The Whole Armor of God

The whole armor of God should be put on daily. There is much dispute over how to put on the armor. Some even ask, "Should I take it off at night while I'm sleeping? After all, in the natural, you don't sleep with armor on." Actually, the armor of

God is put on and kept on. The enemy attacks at night also.

Ephesians 6:13–17 describes six items in the armor. These pieces of armor—the helmet of salvation, the breastplate of righteousness, the shield of faith, the belt of truth, the shoes of the preparation of the Gospel of peace, and the sword of the Spirit need to be understood and appropriated in your spirit. It is Jesus Christ who is our armor. Jesus Christ is our salvation, our righteousness, the Author, Finisher, and object of our faith, our truth, our readiness, our Prince of Peace, our Sword, and the Word of God.

No believer would be able to claim that the armor goes on just by the saying. The stronger the spiritual walk, the stronger the armor. The armor covers not from the outside but from inside, in the spirit. We need to be full-time warriors, not just weekend warriors, as the National Guard is often called. Therefore, the armor is perpetual. We are no longer civilians. As soon as we become born-again Christians, we enter into spiritual warfare. Perpetual armor means a perpetual walk in righteousness and holiness. You need to be right with God daily. Maintain a humbleness and a meekness built on repentance and daily seeking of Him.

The Word of God

The Sword of the Spirit, which is the Word of God, represents one of the few offensive weapons in our arsenal. But praise God, it provides all that we need, for the Word contains every spiritual weapon.

Speak the Word in faith and it becomes yours. Every deliverance worker must have the Word of God at the tip of his tongue. Not knowing the Word is like leaving your weapons at home. Demons hate hearing the Word, especially those Scriptures that tell about their defeat. It is impossible to list all warfare Scriptures since the entire Bible applies, but we frequently say the following:

- We have been given all authority to tread on serpents and scorpions, and over all the power of the enemy. Nothing shall by any means hurt us (Luke 10:19).
- Jesus has defeated you. He spoiled principalities and made a show of them openly, triumphing over them. He took away the keys to hell and death (Col. 2:15; Rev. 1:18).
- And these signs shall follow them that believe. In my name shall they cast out demons (Mark 16:17).
- And He gave them power over demons to cast them out. The word of God is quick, and powerful, and sharper than any two-edged sword, piercing even to the dividing asunder of soul and spirit. I hereby divide and separate this person's soul from his spirit and turn over complete control of soul and spirit to our Lord Jesus.
- Listen to the Word of God, demon. Matthew 16:19 says that whatsoever I bind on earth shall be bound in heaven and whatsoever I loose on earth shall be loosed in heaven. I now bind the strongman of Pride (or other) over this person in Jesus' name. I cut off all cords between you and any other spirit in this person.
- The entire chapter of Isaiah 47.
- The entire chapter of Revelation 18.

- The entire chapter of Revelation 20.
- Greater is He who is in me than he who is in the world (1 John. 4:4).
- He who has the keys of David, what door he closes, none shall open; and what door he opens, none shall close (Rev. 3:7).
- I have been cleansed by the blood of Jesus The blood cleanses (Rev. 1:5).
- The Lord will cause a drought to be upon her waters (Jer. 50:38; 51:36). I will dry up her sea, and make her springs dry.
- I dry up your river, even as the Jordan was dried up and the people of God went into the promised land on dry ground (Josh. 3:16).
- I dry up your roots even as the Lord Jesus dried up the fig tree (Matt. 21:19).
- I knock down your two-leaved gates and the gates shall not be shut. I break in pieces your gates of brass and cut in sunder the bars of iron (Isa. 45:1–2).
- I break down your walls even, as the walls of Jericho came tumbling down (Josh. 6:5).
- I bind up the strongman in the heavens over this person (or church, area, house, family, et cetera) in the name of Jesus. We have all authority to bind you up, for the Lord said, *"Whatsoever ye shall bind on earth shall be bound in heaven: and whatsoever ye shall loose on earth shall be loosed in heaven"* (Matt. 18:18).
- We cut off your cords (Ps. 129:4). We cast them away.
- We break all curses of iniquity coming down the family line on the mother's side and the father's side, ten generations backwards and forwards.
- We claim our Lord Jesus Christ as our curse, for it is

written, *"Christ hath redeemed us from the curse of the law, being made a curse for us: for it is written, Cursed is everyone that hangeth on a tree"* (Gal. 3:13).

- We command you to bend your knee to Jesus and to confess that Jesus is Lord, for it is written, *"That at the name of Jesus every knee should bow, of things in heaven, and things in earth, and things under the earth; and that every tongue should confess that Jesus Christ is Lord, to the glory of God the Father"* (Phil. 2:10–11).

- I put a hook in your nose, a cord around your tongue, and I bore a thorn in your jaw (Job 41). (This is a very effective Scripture when you're up against a serpent, which is quite often.)

When fighting against Jezebel, the primary chapters are Isaiah 47, Revelation 17, and Revelation 18. You can extract verses or read the whole passage to them. The following sequence has been used many times:

- I take away your throne and I destroy it in the name of Jesus. I command you to sit in the dust. You are no queen. You are no virgin. Neither are you tender and delicate. You're just an old hag (Isa. 47:1).

- You are common. Grind meal, uncover your locks, make bare the leg, uncover the thigh, pass over the rivers. You are exposed (Isa. 47:2–3).

- You're no queen. Bow your knee.

Many other warfare Scriptures deserve memorizing. You don't have to memorize it exactly, but you cannot twist the meaning of it. Demons know when you misquote.

Often, stubborn spirits leave when I read Revelation chapter twenty to them. Again, what works in one case may not work in another.

I cannot overemphasize the importance of memorizing Scripture. Rebecca Brown relates an incident she had one dark night when a group of satanists surrounded her home and started sending curses and evil spirits to the inhabitants of her house. For two hours she sat in total darkness and quoted Scriptures one after another. As she continued to quote warfare and praise Scriptures, the enemy was unable to come in, and the waves of evil sent against the occupants gradually faded away. The two young women in the home who did not know Scripture . felt defenseless and terrified (Brown, *He Came to Set the Captives Free,* 213–230; 270–271).

Pride

The deliverance worker must always be careful that Pride does not creep into him or her. It is so easy to become proud when you see demons flee. You start to think that you are very powerful and anointed. The demons know, and God knows. Once, a deliverance worker felt quite proud of herself. Though often instructed to rid herself of the spirit of Pride, she never did. During a deliverance session, she hopped over to assist by praying on the side. The demons laughed and said to her, "Don't make me laugh. You're so full of pride, you can't get any of us out. We've got you. Ha, Ha, Ha." The woman's face became as red as a beet. She was so befuddled and embarrassed that she left in a huff. Needless to say, a deliverance session with her for Pride was in order.

Pride erodes your walk with God. God knows exactly what's in your heart. It's the Holy Spirit that delivers and the blood of Jesus that gives us the victory. Whenever we think it is by our own power and holiness, we stumble. We need to keep ourselves humble before the Lord at all times. No man or woman can say that he or she healed delivered someone. I have never delivered or healed anyone in my life. It was always Jesus, through His Spirit!

Your Spirit

In deliverance we fight in the spirit. For that reason, we need to pay careful attention to the condition of our spirits. Be sensitive to your spirit. Is it normal? Do you feel oppressed, weak, or dry? Perhaps it is demonically oppressed. Perhaps it needs more attention in the area of prayer, reading of the Word, fasting, or obedience. Perhaps your daily activities overtire your body. The physical conditions of our bodies sometimes affect our spirits and vice versa. Although we receive strength through the Holy Spirit, the condition of the human body affects the working of the spirit. As the spirit needs to be kept on an even keel, so it is with the body. Over excitement puts it out of kilter. Often, after a night of fighting in the spirit against demons I find it difficult to sleep. If you also experience sleeplessness, one cure for that is prayer, especially praying in tongues. It quiets the mind and spirit.

Like any athlete, the spirit must be exercised. It gets lazy quite easily. For that reason, I make it a practice to get involved in a deliverance session at least once a week, although it's not always possible. Shadow boxing or reading a book on boxing cannot match getting into a ring and exchanging punches with a real adversary. You find out rather quickly how ineffective some of your pet ideas are. Your imagined killer punch turns out to be a powder puff. You also find out what works. Theory and doctrine must be put into practice; otherwise they are hollow words.

The apostle James says it nicely in James 2:14: *"What doth it profit, my brethren, though a man say he hath faith, and have not works? can faith save him?"* Again, the apostle says:

> *Even so faith, if it hath not works, is dead, being alone. Yea, a man may say, Thou hast faith, and I have works: show me thy faith without thy works, and I will show thee my faith by my works.* (James 2:17–18)

In verse twenty, James says, *"But wilt thou know, O vain man, that faith without works is dead?"* Deliverance tests a man's faith, the same as divine healing or raising the dead. As you go from one deliverance to another, your faith starts to build, and your works become more profitable.

Although the Holy Spirit provides the power behind every deliverance session, your mind translates what the Spirit says through intuition. So long as your mind is submitted to the Spirit, you will move powerfully against the enemy. Cooperation between your mind and the Spirit improves with use. When workers move in this realm, it is beautiful. As the writer of the book of Hebrews says in chapter five verse fourteen, *"But strong meat belongeth to them that are of full age, even those who by reason of use have their senses exercised to discern both good and evil."* In order to develop your spirit, you need to exercise it through use.

The Deliverance Team

A well-trained deliverance team is wonderful. Even when the members come from different teams, their familiarity with teamwork aids in the process. A team usually varies in size from three to six. In the case of a violent manifestation, a larger team is better. It often requires six people to hold a person down when the demons intend to kick and bite.

The team should have a designated leader and an assistant leader or two. The leader opens the session with prayer and directs the deliverance vocally. The assistant backs up the leader with Scripture, prayer, and agreement. The rest pray in tongues and agree. As the battle rages, the entire team waits upon the Lord for discernment and instructions and relays them to the leaders. When the leader tires, someone jumps in to take his place. The leader moves forward until he feels tired or someone else's discernment or anointing indicates that he or she should take over. When coordination is lacking, the battle becomes confused. One may be calling out one spirit and another calling out an entirely different demon.

Avoid strife and envy among team workers. God uses one and then the other in most deliverance sessions. Often a heavy anointing is on one person in the team while praying for an individual, and then the anointing shifts to another during the same session or one following soon thereafter.

The Place and Other Details

Choose a place away from homes or locations where the general public may misunderstand what is going on. Often demons scream at the top of their voices, and quite frankly it sometimes sounds like a rape or beating. Police officers sometimes appear at inopportune moments, and you may find it difficult to explain why six people are holding down a screaming and thrashing woman.

A male should avoid delivering a woman unless her husband, boyfriend, or other women assist or attend. Some mentally unbalanced women may otherwise cry rape. Carelessness could easily ruin a deliverance ministry. Satan doesn't need much more than a little opening to execute his dirty work. Even the most ethical male medical doctors never attempt to examine a female patient unless another female is present.

Tell women not to wear low-cut dresses or blouses to a deliverance session. They should wear jeans, if possible. They should also wear undergarments. The same applies to deliverance workers. Impromptu wrestling matches between workers and possessed people may provide some embarrassing incidents. When demons take over the actions of a person, they spit, scream, claw, and bite. Although this is not the norm, it happens often enough. Even when the woman merely sits down on a chair, her movements sometimes make it difficult for male workers calling the demons out. You don't know where to look when the demon starts struggling and contorting her body.

You need to keep blankets on the premises in order to cover the women who are struggling on the ground. When overtaken by demons who want to kick and scratch, place them on their stomachs. If they continue struggling, sitting on a chair presents dangerous possibilities for them such as falling and hitting their heads on the chair or floor.

In some cases, demons will attempt to hurt the person being delivered by causing him to lift his head and pound it on the cement floor. Obviously, it is wise to cover the floor with carpet or a rug. It hurts even on a carpeted floor, and you may need to hold his or her head above the ground. Make sure that he or she does not bite your hands or arms. A person on his or her back finds spitting, biting, and kicking the workers easier. On his face, he loses most of that opportunity. Should he be placed on his face, slide newspapers under the chin. If not, he could skin his nose, elbow, and chin on the carpet as he thrashes about.

If you suspect that a person's propensity to violence or anger will result in a struggle, instruct him or her strongly to stay in control. Sometimes, the demons manifest so strongly that the person cannot control her actions, although this seldom happens. God protects His workers, but it would be sheer folly not to be prepared. Never stand squarely in front of a sitting person being delivered. A well placed kick will incapacitate any worker. I've never seen bad injuries to a person being delivered, although I've seen people bruised from struggling.

However, I've seen deliverance workers injured because of failure to prepare or be aware. It is surprising how foolish people can be in dealing with demons. They allow the person complete freedom to punch, kick, spit, claw, and bite. Be cautious. It takes only a split second. Of course, in many instances, God mercifully heals any injuries that take place in a deliverance session. Foresight and wisdom will save the day in most cases.

I once helped pray for a Pentecostal pastor who was about 6'3" and weighed over 250 pounds. He was such a gentle person, we figured he would never blow up. He did. He raised his knee and broke three of my ribs in one movement that took half a second. The ensuing three months of pain provided a valuable lesson. God healed me, but He took His time about it to teach me a lesson. Be prepared.

In most instances, people can prevent their own uncontrolled demonstrations. Remind the person sharply if you have to. Demons will steal away the testimony of a person who is out of control.

In one case, a young woman started trembling and getting physically out of control not only during a deliverance session but also praise sessions or when the presence of God was strong. During one particular church service, the Holy Spirit moved powerfully, and she started shaking all over. This time we insisted that she maintain control by claiming her authority and power by the blood of Jesus. After a few moments, the manifestations subsided. She later confessed that she so feared that demons would manifest by shaking and trembling that she refused to play praise tapes or praise God when no one was around. After her triumph over the demons, she lost her fear and hesitation. She knew her authority over the demons. They never manifested during inopportune times again.

I've also found that when a person forces herself to stay in control of her body and mind, the demons weaken and flee.

Frequently, you find women competing in the area of manifestations. One woman in church goes through a yelling and screaming manifestation, and the next woman wants to go one better. It indicates Spiritual Pride and a Jezebel spirit. Each wants to be better than the other. They compete with each other through their demons screaming and swearing louder than anyone else's. Be aware of games that demons play. Invariably, it is the work of the Jezebel spirit who does not want to be outdone.

With some men, the spirit of Poor Me rises up by creating a tantrum where the spirit attempts to hurt other people. It's like a little child looking for attention. You may notice that more women than men put on demonstrations. In fact, more women submit for deliverance. Men have an image to keep which prevents them from being transparent. The Ahab spirit in men, of course, will cause them to hang back and not get delivered. When you look at the fruits in their lives, however, they are negative and often devastating. They may feel that nothing is the matter with them, but they haven't had steady jobs for years, are on the verge of divorces, and are known to get drunk. They owe money to many, and family situations are miserable. Of course, they blame it all on circumstances and other people. Obviously you should encourage such people to receive deliverance.

God allows trials and afflictions to touch the saints. If afflicted by illness or other problems for a long time, it may be that God wants to get their attention on certain areas of their lives that are unpleasing to God. You can't go on sinning and expect deliverance. Neither can you allow certain areas to go unchanged and expect deliverance. People want deliverance from all kinds of problems which are actually not so much caused by demons as much as weak wills. You can't blame demons for everything.

Basically, many marginal Christians hold back full commitment and obedience to God. They still want to do their own things. They either have a difficult time with deliverance or if delivered, will soon be back worse than before. It's like a man coming in for deliverance from Sexual Lust who then goes home to his live-in girlfriend. Some people think that if they get rid of demons, their problems disappear. They forget that they still live in bodies of flesh. The desires and passions of the flesh are always present and have to be put down daily, with or without demons. There is a law of sin in the flesh, and it's not all demons (Rom. 7:23).

When deliverance or healing doesn't seem to be working, something is blocking it, or God's will is that the deliverance or healing not take place at that time. God is not the author of illness. He is the Lord that heals us, and although He may permit Satan to touch our bodies where Satan has a right, it is always for a particular reason. God wants other things changed first. Perhaps a splintered pride or a bad family relationship, unforgiveness, bitterness, or love of self prevent healing or deliverance. No two cases are exactly alike. You need to ask for wisdom from God.

The main thrust of this chapter is Mark 16:17, *"And these signs shall follow them that believe; In my name shall they cast out devils."* If you are a believer, you shall cast out demons in the name of Jesus. There are no exceptions.

Abuse of Power

Deliverance is a very powerful ministry. Unfortunately, we sometimes hear of pastors abusing their authority. They masquerade as all-knowing and all-powerful leaders who are anointed in a special way by God. They place their people under bondage by demanding that every little thing in their congregations' lives be controlled by church leadership, even the decision as to what kind of automobiles to purchase, what schools to attend, and whom to marry. Deliverance gives an appearance of power and favor with God when in actuality, every Christian has an unction from the Holy Spirit to cast out demons.

We've heard how some pastors use a basic knowledge of deliverance to place their people in fear so that they can be manipulated. In one case aired on national television, a pastor used his so-called deliverance knowledge and power to convince a wife that she must engage in illicit sex with him as part of deliverance therapy. I abhor and denounce any such manipulation and dishonesty. Such leaders will taste the wrath of God. Deliverance is built on love and compassion, not on personal lust for power and control. I realize that such leaders emerge in many other ministries, deliverance or otherwise. They prey on the ignorance and fear of others and devour the sheep.

Deliverance leaders should always minister in love and concern, never in greed or lust. Without love, all of your efforts will be worthless (1 Cor. 13:1–3). Be extra careful to maintain a faultless ministry, devoid of any suspicion and completely open to others. Walk in the truth.

Chapter Eleven

Preparing the Person to Be Delivered

P re-deliverance counseling may save much time and make the difference between success and failure. All sessions are successful in the sense that it brings some benefit. At the very least, it could lead to a conclusion that the person should not be delivered yet.

Thorough counseling should include the following:

- Inform the person being delivered what to expect.
- Deliverance is not a pill or a panacea for everything. The deliveree must fall out of agreement with demons. He needs to know what lies he has accepted from the enemy and what sins he is committing that continue to keep him in bondage. You'd be surprised how many Christians believe that living with a girlfriend is acceptable.

- The deliveree needs to know that demons do not cause all of his afflictions. He brings many upon himself. God allows some in order to bring some area of his life to his attention. Sometimes the person needs to learn how to carry his cross. Deliverance may cast out the demon, but one still needs to learn how to walk in dominion. Overcoming involves both deliverance and living by the Word of God.
- Repentance still stands out as one of the most important elements in the Christian walk. Sin gives demons legal rights to torment. The deliverance counselor should run through the list of legal rights given by God to Satan and his workers. As you go down the list, start breaking down the legal rights and strongholds. If the person resists confession of sin and repentance, deliverance becomes senseless. Deliverance represents a form of cleansing (*"Be thou clean"* Matt. 8:3), and confession and repentance precede God's forgiveness. Demons know their rights and refuse to come out if there are areas of unforgiven sin.
- Counseling should be designed to create a better relationship between the deliveree and the workers. We don't need to be super-spiritual in order to discern spirits. A mere excursion into a person's life history will quickly reveal areas of demonic invasion. If the person or his family played with witchcraft, for instance, it doesn't take much discernment to realize that occultic spirits and curses probably control.

- Counsel the person on what he should do after deliverance. Make it clear that deliverance is not a one-shot deal. Neither is salvation. When God prepared the Hebrew nation to conquer the promised land, He informed them that He would not conquer their enemies in one year, "*lest the land become desolate, and the beast of the field multiply against thee*" (Exod. 23:29). When the person is ready, God will cause him to be delivered of the next stronghold. Meanwhile, the person needs to remain under the covering of authority and fellowship. He needs to fill up the empty places from the former habitation of a cast-out spirit with the Word of God and righteousness and not invite spirits back in (Matt. 12:43–45).

What a person says may be far from the truth. Discernment, when it is truly from God, is never wrong. Some will say that they have forgiven, but in actuality they haven't. In one case, a young man insisted that he had forgiven his parents for their trespasses against him. Later in the same conversation, he commented that he hadn't seen his parents for years. They lived close by, but he never wanted to talk to them. "I forgive them, but I don't want to have anything to do with them." He had not truly forgiven them.

In some cases, a person needs to know his or her role in the original sin. Often, a person is unforgiving because he doesn't want to face his own involvement and guilt to begin with. A person can avoid responsibility in the trespass by steadfastly blaming others. A woman who had to marry because she got pregnant may blame the husband: "He forced me." God wants a clean heart, not a deceptive one.

Often, the person seeking deliverance needs to get with God and ask that areas of unforgiveness be revealed. God will surely answer a sincere person.

Desire

Does the person really want the spirit out? He may say yes, but deep inside he doesn't. For instance, many young men want to have Sexual Lust controlled but not eliminated completely. They think it a good idea to slow down their sexual desires, but only when these desires cannot be satisfied. They don't really want to give up their fantasies and porno films.

Does the person really desire to walk with the Lord, or does he want a quick fix? Does he want major surgery or just an aspirin? If he desires deliverance out of religious pride alone, then deliverance may be impossible. Selfishness and pride can block any moving of the Holy Spirit. God will not be mocked. I recall times when people came to church with a "show me" attitude. So long as they stood around, nothing happened. As soon as they left the building, the Spirit moved and tremendous deliverance took place. God knows exactly what to do and when.

Is he acting? Is he going through deliverance to show how sincere he is, to be accepted by his peers, or does he really want to be made clean? You may need to show the person the true ugliness of the demons and how they control his life.

If necessary, you should assign someone to disciple and minister to the person on a more constant basis in order to bring more understanding to him. At times, you need to take a harsher approach, in love, in order to shake him up. Complacency among Christians puts a chill on the movement of the Holy Spirit.

Not a Quick Fix

The church is not a supermarket where people can come in for a quick pickup. Some people want demons out but don't want Jesus in. If the person attends church regularly, it sometimes profits you to question his walk with God. If the person neither attends church nor intends to, it would be better not to pray deliverance over him unless he is inclined to accept Jesus.

Some people don't really want Jesus. They just want a better life without changing anything. They come in to have curses broken in order to make more money, get a better job or girlfriend, find a lover, get married, or have a better life. Leave them alone unless they make that decision to walk with Jesus. They accept Jesus and yet reject Him as their personal Savior. People are so selfish in their motives sometimes.

You see, even if you get the demons out, they come back again. The Word says that when you cast a demon out, he goes through the dry places and, finding no rest, returns and seeing his former habitation empty, swept clean, and garnished, he brings back with him seven demons more wicked than him.

Then the latter state of the person is worse than the former (Matt. 12:43–45). It is absolutely true. Therefore, do them a favor, and don't deliver them if they refuse to walk in holiness or do not show signs of wanting to be converted. Their latter condition will be worse than their former.

One person came for deliverance, but she did not really intend to walk with God; she just wanted to be rid of her boyfriend. However, because of her Sexual Lust spirits, she found it difficult to refuse his sexual advances, and, therefore, they ended up together time and again. After getting the lust spirits out, she did not continue to attend church and she ended up back in the world. As a result, she found herself more promiscuous and full of lust than ever before. When she finally came back, we challenged her as to her motives. After a while, she desired a pure walk with Jesus. Jesus set her free, and she now enjoys a Christian walk free of sexual problems.

Certainly, the devil tries to come back every so often and entice you, even after the demons leave. Every Christian must learn to stand and resist when that happens. Getting demons out does not mean freedom from temptation forever. Even with our Lord Jesus, Satan left only for a season (Luke 4:13).

On the other hand, when you discern that people are open to receive Jesus, deliverance may lead them to salvation. Signs and wonders follow the preaching of the Gospel in order to confirm the Word. The signs and wonders cause unbelievers to believe. In that particular situation, deliverance may convince fence straddlers that Jesus lives.

Counseling

A person's history can uncover areas such as negative soul ties and occult involvement. Such knowledge can eliminate a lot of wasted time trying to receive spiritual discernment as to the identification of the spirits involved. Family roots reveal plenty. If mother married three times, you don't need much discernment to recognize Rejection and possibly Jezebel. If an ancestor was a convicted murderer, it's obvious what you're up against. If a parent once practiced witchcraft, it doesn't take much discernment to know what spirits lurk in the shadows. You don't need to play psychiatrist, but digging into a person's history and personal background may save you time.

Counseling helps in preparing the person in connection with what to expect and how to react. Sometimes, lack of preparation leaves a person bewildered and embarrassed. If a person does not want certain people at the session, you need to know why. Often a person is embarrassed to confess to sexual lust, masturbation, fantasy, or fornication. If he hesitates because of certain people present, it may hinder the deliverance. Protect the person being delivered.

The person should be informed not to pray or think of any particular thing during deliverance. Otherwise, he may block out the demons' manifestations Sometimes, it helps to have the person speak out loud the thoughts going through his mind, even if they involve swearing. Once exposed in that fashion, the demons can be commanded to leave. Some deliverance ministries claim that it glorifies Satan to allow demons to speak. Others feel that all demons are liars anyway. Regardless, I find it necessary in a fair number of cases.

Jesus engaged in conversations with demons; they came out of people with loud cries, and demons occasionally manifested themselves physically. In Mark 5:2–13, Jesus not only commanded the demons to leave, He also asked them their names. The Bible says that the demons, *"besought him much that he would not send them away out of the country"* (v. 10). The word *"much"* indicates that the conversation was more than salutatory. Jesus did not try to quiet them. (See also Luke 8:27–34.) In Mark 1:25, Jesus commanded the demons to hold their peace. However, this command implies that Jesus did not want the demons to reveal His identity as the Messiah yet, although Jesus did not object to other statements since the next verse says, *"And when the unclean spirit had torn him, and cried with a loud voice, he came out of him."* "Tearing" shows that the demon manifested itself by doing things to the man's body. The demon cried in a loud voice. In deliverance, demons often cry out and cause the body of the person being delivered to go into various contortions, although this is relatively rare (Acts 8:7).

Mark 1:34 answers the question of why Jesus told the demons to hold their peace. It says, *"And he healed many that were sick of divers diseases, and cast out many devils; and suffered not the devils to speak, because they knew him."* Jesus did not want to be revealed as the Messiah yet.

> *Devils also came out of many, crying out, and*
> *saying, Thou art Christ the Son of God. And he*
> *rebuking them suffered them not to speak: for*
> *they knew that he was Christ.* (Luke 4:41)

Later episodes of casting out demons do not indicate that Jesus commanded the demons to "*hold thy peace*" (Mark 1:25).

In Mark 9:26, Jesus cast out a deaf and dumb spirit. "*And the spirit cried, and rent him sore, and came out of him: and he was as one dead; insomuch that many said, He is dead.*" This sentence shows three things: first, the spirit made a noise; second, it did something to the boy's body; third, many people observed it.

Inform the deliveree not to suppress the demons or their manifestation. He or she should cooperate with the deliverers by speaking out anything that they hear or feel like saying. It may be a demon speaking or giving the feeling, and expressing it helps to expose the demon.

Mass deliverance or group deliverance refers to the calling out of demons by one (or more) person(s) to a crowd of people of varying numbers. Some deliverance ministries use mass deliverance quite effectively. Others claim mass deliverance glorifies the devil and should not be done on the following grounds: (1) it embarrasses the person delivered; (2) it frightens the onlookers; (3) it promotes violence and allows demons to scream obscenities or act up; (4) it is unbiblical because Jesus did not allow demons to talk. Opponents of mass deliverance (let's call them "private counselors") claim that certain forms of witchcraft involve very powerful spirits that may cause havoc in mass deliverance.

Private counselors favor closed sessions on a one-to-one basis where the person giving deliverance assists the person receiving deliverance in the area of repentance and self-deliverance.

Mass deliverers claim that if a person truly repents and desires to be set free, he or she should not mind being in the company of believers and other people seeking God. If embarrassment prevents someone from going forward, then perhaps he doesn't want it bad enough. In fact, some mass deliverers totally refuse to give private counseling on the ground that it is usually pride that makes a person want special attention.

Mass deliverance can reach a greater number of people and rarely gets out of hand. I've conducted mass deliverance sessions to as many as six hundred and fifty saints at one time. People observing mass deliverance receive a boast to their faith in God when they hear and see demons manifesting. It convinces many that Jesus is Lord.

Those with closed session counseling ministries seem to be dealing mostly with Satan worshippers who come to them singly or with mental patients that do not come en masse to receive deliverance. It is true that Satan worshippers often have very powerful and ugly demons, and one should not allow such demons to manifest since it is likely that the onlookers will become frightened. Further, mental patients often need counseling just to give them enough courage and understanding to stand against the powers of darkness.

Self-Deliverance

Some advocate teaching the person how to deliver himself. He is taught to command the spirits in his own body to leave. Of course, this is important; however, again you need wisdom. There are certain spirits that are too powerful to get out through self-deliverance, or it may depend on the degree of maturity the Christian has.

God Is Still the Boss

In the very end, we must conclude that God works in many different ways. To one deliverance worker, the Holy Spirit may require one-on-one sessions. With another, the Holy Spirit blesses mass deliverance. In every instance, the Holy Spirit should be in control. There have been times when mass deliverance does not work for someone but private counseling does. Sometimes group deliverance forces a particular demon to manifest, but it refuses to leave. When that particular person is worked on privately, the demons leave. One should not be rigid or limit the Holy Spirit in either extreme. I've worked both ends of the spectrum and the middle also. Very often, instead of having either mass deliverance or private sessions, I ask those who desire to be prayed over to sit in the front row of seats, and we assign teams of three or four to work with them.

I can recall times when the Holy Spirit just sovereignly effected mass deliverance. Sometimes when teaching deliverance, people in the audience start choking and coughing. Pretty soon a half-dozen or more received deliverance without any human assistance. At that point, mass deliverance takes place almost automatically. At other times, I think that the Holy Spirit desires mass deliverance, yet there is no confirmation or movement, so I abandon the idea. However, as we go into semi-private prayer, the Spirit moves. *"Not by might, nor by power, but by my spirit saith the LORD of hosts"* (Zech. 4:6).

We need to be sensitive to the Holy Spirit and follow whatever He says. Once you start observing a rigid formula or sequence, you take away the Holy Spirit's right to lead. I'm not saying that you should not follow a pattern; just be constantly aware of what the Spirit is saying in each case.

Chapter Twelve

Anatomy of a Deliverance

No two deliverances will be exactly alike. However, the sequence below epitomizes a typical deliverance session. I present it so that you may obtain some insight into what may happen during deliverance. This knowledge will hopefully eliminate undue fear and apprehension in people desiring to enter the deliverance ministry or to effect a deliverance.

A Practice Run

Let me set the stage. Joan is a woman around twenty-six years old who innocently delved into the occult when a friend introduced her to ouija boards and Dungeons and Dragons at the age of fifteen. She has difficulty holding a job and finds herself depressed and suicidal. She had a fight with her boyfriend eight months ago and is bitter about it. They broke up, and she cannot talk with him without yelling and crying. She recently became a born-again Christian and was baptized in the Holy Spirit. She tries to pray and read her Bible but falls asleep as soon as she starts praying or reading the Word. Whenever she prays in tongues, she eventually starts to yell, swear, and guttural words of anger come out of her mouth.

First, you need to counsel Joan, if possible. If not possible because of circumstances of time and place, you need to at least give her an idea of what to expect during a deliverance session. (Refer to the chapter "Preparing a Person for Deliverance.")

Second, I am assuming that the people conducting the deliverance have prepared themselves through prayer and fasting, if necessary. In most cases, a Christian who walks daily in Christ need not go through any special regimen or preparation.

Sit the person on a comfortable chair. One worker can sit on either side of her. Do not stand or sit directly in front of her, as she could kick or strike unexpectedly. Inform Joan that she is to refrain and restrain herself from biting, kicking, punching, or other physically harmful actions.

> **Worker:** Let's start off with a word of prayer. Father, we come to you with the precious blood of our Lord Jesus Christ, and we claim your protection. We put on the whole armor of God—the helmet of salvation, the breastplate of righteousness, the shield of faith, the belt of truth, the shoes of the preparation of the Gospel of peace, and the sword of the Spirit. We put on the Lord Jesus Christ, for the Word of God says that He is our salva-

tion, our righteousness, the object of our faith, and the author and finisher of our faith, as well as our readiness. Our Lord Jesus is also the Prince of Peace. He is our peace. The sword of the Spirit is the Word of God, and Jesus Christ is the Word of God.

We ask that you send your warring angels, that you place a hedge of fire about us to keep the enemy out, that you ring us round about with your angels, Lord. We lift up Joan to you and ask that you set her free from these demons that have placed her in bondage. We thank you for it in Jesus' Name. Amen.

There is no rigid requirement that an opening prayer has to be like the above.

Worker: Now, Joan, we want you to renounce out loud involvement in the occult, or any other sins that the Holy Spirit brings to mind. Ask God to forgive you. (Lead her through the prayer below.)

Joan: Lord, I renounce all involvement in the occult. I declare to Satan that I belong to Jesus Christ, and He is my Lord and Savior. I renounce all involvement in ouija boards, fortune-telling, Dungeons and Dragons, palm-reading, and any form of witchcraft. Father, I repent for having participated in any occult activities, and I ask for your forgiveness. I claim the blood of Jesus over my life.

Worker: Joan, you need to forgive your boyfriend, parents, brothers, sisters, and anyone that you have any grievances against or problems with. (Once again, lead her.)

Joan: Father, I forgive my boyfriend for

leaving me and for the many things that I have held against him. I ask that you help me to completely accept him. I forgive my mother and father for not helping me and for the things that I have held against them. Lord, I do not wish to have any bitterness in my life. Lord, I ask that you now forgive me my sins.

Have Joan speak them out loud, but not so anyone can hear, if it is of the nature that may hurt or embarrass anyone, including Joan. Actually, I favor having Joan be more specific in the areas which she needs to forgive.

Worker: Father, we stand with Joan, and we ask that your kind mercies be extended to her as your child. In the name of Jesus Christ of Nazareth, we break all curses of iniquity that have come down Joan's family line, back ten generations on each side of her family, her mother's side and her father's side. We claim our Lord Jesus Christ as her curse, for it is written in the Word of God that Jesus served as a curse for us, that everyone who hangeth from a tree is cursed. Father, we pray forgiveness for the sins of her forefathers.

Lord, you have heard Joan forgive all those that have trespassed against her, we ask that you break all curses caused by unforgiveness.

We break all soul ties between Joan and her boyfriend in the name of Jesus. We break all soul ties between Joan and her mother. We break all hexes and curses that have been placed on her from all sources, in Jesus name.

If the Holy Spirit prompts you to lay hands on Joan's head or shoulders, you should do so. Otherwise, you should not. Men should not lay hands on a woman below the shoulders, even on her back. If the female subject or other woman lays hands on those parts, the men can place their hands on the top of the woman's hand.

> **Worker:** Demons, we call you to attention. We come against you in the name of Jesus. We command that you will not cause any violence or vomiting. We bind up the strongman of Jezebel in the heavenlies. We bind you up hand and foot with chains from heaven. We put a gag in your mouth. We cut off all cords between you and the spirits in Joan. We cast them off. We bind up the spirit of Leviathan in the heavenlies.

Bind up all strongmen the Holy Spirit shows you.

> **Worker:** Demons, we dry up your waters. The Word of God says that He will dry up your seas and cause a drought. We make your habitation a dry desolation. We dry up your seas, your rivers, and your springs. We knock your gates down. The Word of God says that the gates of hell shall not prevail against the church. The Word also says that the Lord will break the two-leaved gates, He will break the bars of brass and cut asunder the bars of iron.
>
> We knock down your pillars. We bind up the gatekeeper of Pride and Witchcraft. We knock down every wall. Not one stone shall

stand upon the other.

We pour the blood of Jesus all over you. It cleanses.

We command you to come out in Jesus, name. We have all authority over you in His name. He has given us all power to tread on serpents and scorpions and over all the power of the enemy. Nothing shall by any means hurt us. I put you under my feet right now in Jesus' name, and I stomp on you.

Greater is He who is in us than he who is in the world. The Lord Jesus has defeated you. He spoiled principalities and made a show of them openly, triumphing over them in it. Jesus defeated Satan himself.

Demon, you are a defeated enemy. We command you to loose this woman. Leave in the name of Jesus. We bind up even Satan in the heavenlies. We cut off all cords between you and Satan.

Your helpers should be agreeing with you and praying in tongues. The assistant should be agreeing with you and more or less echoing your statements or adding some of his own. The assistant should relay what he receives from the Holy Spirit to you.

By this time, the spirits will likely be manifesting and coming out through coughing, vomiting, choking, yawning, or weeping. If not, the person should at least be twitching or claiming cramps in the stomach or shoulders and neck. Command them to manifest and come out. If they still do not, there is some area of legal rights that has not yet been touched. Sometimes, the person has occultic jewelry on his or her person, or there is unforgiveness. Sometimes, there are things in her home that are cursed objects. These need to be taken care of first.

Deliverance always works. If there are no manifestations for ten or fifteen minutes, that indicates areas of rights the demons have.

Commanding the Spirit to Go Back Down

If there is unforgiveness, the person needs to forgive. If you are in the thick of a fight with demons and they are screaming or resisting, use the following sequence:

Worker: Demon, I want to speak to Joan. I command you to go back down. I command you in Jesus' name to release Joan and go back down until I call you. I want to speak to Joan. Joan, are you here? Say, "Jesus is Lord."

If the person cannot say "Jesus is Lord," the demons have not yet gone down. Keep commanding them to go back down. Sometimes they resist, but if you keep insisting, they will have to go back down. In the case of particularly strong ruling demons, it may take five minutes to force them to go back down; however, I have never had a case where they did not. When the person acknowledges that Jesus is Lord, his voice will usually indicate that he has regained control. Instruct him to forgive whomever the Holy Spirit has shown you. If he refuses, the session ends right there. If he cooperates and immediately forgives out loud, you may go right back into battle.

Worker: Spirit, you heard. She has forgiven her friend. She has broken your legal hold. I command you to come out in Jesus' name.

Usually, the demons will come out quickly at that point. If not, there is another legal right somewhere. Ask God to reveal it. Once the legal right is renounced and broken, demons must leave. There are no exceptions.

Different Techniques

There are many other weapons in the Spirit. Different workers favor different techniques. Some favor fires from heaven or coals of fire heaped on heads. Some favor the sword of God, arrows, lances, or hail stones. Personally, I have had great success with the blood of Jesus. Demons cannot resist the blood.

When working against specific spirits such as Leviathan, use the weapons given by the Word. Leviathan is vulnerable to the breaking of its heads by the sword of the Lord, to a hook in the nose, a thorn in the jaw, and a cord around the tongue. Since Leviathan is described as a crooked and piercing serpent, I ask God to straighten Leviathan out and to pull him out of every deep place.

Other weapons include asking God to send His hornets into the land to search out every demon. Often, the demons will start crying out as if a hornet has stung them. Ask God to shine His light into every dark corner. Demons hate light.

Sometimes, we stand on the Word that says, *"Where two or three are gathered in my name, there am I in the midst of them*" (Matt. 18:20). We declare the Word, and ask Jesus to be in our midst and to show the demons where to go. Then we say, "Demon, Jesus has shown you where to go. We command you to go where Jesus sends you."

Although some churches claim that once you have commanded the spirits to come out, it is automatically over. I beg to differ. The Bible says that we have to "wrestle." The word "wrestle" means to grapple at close quarters. In deliverance, we fight the demons out with more than a simple prayer. Of course, God is sovereign and can deliver a person instantly. However, those cases remain rare. Most of the time, we wrestle and struggle until the demons leave. They leave after arguing and with noises and physical manifestations.

Philip, who was only a deacon, became known for the miracles God did through him.

> *And the people with one accord gave heed unto those things which Philip spake, hearing and seeing the miracles which he did. For unclean spirits, crying with loud voice, came out of many that were possessed with them.*
>
> (Acts 8:6–7)

If You Know the Evil Spirit

If you know the identity of a particular spirit, you may use the Word of God specifically referring to that demon. For instance, during deliverance, the person sometimes will grasp his stomach and lower abdomen, especially in the case of Jezebel. Jezebel loves to inhabit the reproductive organs of women. She also hides in the marrow of the bone, especially the backbone. Jezebel causes painful menstruation, and women with that spirit often miscarry and have a difficult time becoming pregnant. When cast out, the woman stops suffering even from cramps. When casting out Jezebel, we sometimes use the following sequence:

> **Worker**: Jezebel, we stand against you in Jesus' name. We bind up the ruling spirit of Jezebel in the heavenlies. It is written in the Word of God that whatsoever I bind on earth shall be bound in heaven. Whatsoever I loose on earth shall be loosed in heaven. I bind up Jezebel with chains from heaven. Father, we ask that you send warring angels from heaven to help us cast out this ugly spirit.
>
> Jezebel, we command you to sit in the dust. Be common. There is no throne. You are no queen; you are common. You are a liar. You are not a virgin; you are a whore. You are not tender and delicate; you are an ugly, wrinkled, old hag (Isa. 47:1). We take away and destroy all idols and all sacrifices. There shall be no sacrifice.
>
> We command you to take the millstone and to grind meal. Remove your veil, uncover your locks, lift up the skirt, bare the thigh, and cross over the rivers. We expose your nakedness, we expose your shame. We come in the name of the Lord of Israel, the Lord of Hosts.
>
> I dry up your seas, I cause a drought, I dry up your rivers, your springs. There is no

water. It is dry (Jer. 50:38; 51:36).

I knock down your gates. The Lord promises His children that He will go before us so that gates will not be shut. He will shatter the doors of bronze and cut the bars of iron (Isa. 45:1–2). I knock down your pillars. I knock down your walls. Not one stone shall stand upon another.

Flee to the isle of Chittim, you will find no rest. You are defeated. There is no strength in the seas. Your merchants mourn over you. Your city is destroyed. The smoke rises up to heaven, even as with Sodom and Gomorrah. You are defeated. Your young men are destroyed. You shall become a widow in one hour. You shall suffer loss of children. The Lord says He will toss you into a bed and burn you with fire. I pour the blood of Jesus all over you. It cleanses.

Sometimes I read Revelation 18, 20, 21, and 22 to the spirits; they hate it and become weak. Fight with the Word of God, the sword of the Spirit. The Old Testament, as well as the New Testament, is a war manual full of weapons and strategies.

Jezebel loves to hide in the innermost chambers of a person's body and soul. You may need to cut her off from her Ahab husband and from her children for the person to be freed.

Worker: I cut off all cords between (Alice) and her husband, and I cast them away. I cut off all cords between (Alice) and her children and cast them away. There shall be no child sacrifice.

Jezebel will generally wail and scream during deliverance. Occult spirits wail, and she is the queen of witchcraft. She may become violent and try to bite, scratch, and punch. Bind her up and strongly command the person being delivered to stay in control and refrain from violence. "Stop it, Alice. Stay in control. Fight back. Take back control of your mind and body."

Witchcraft steals away fragments of the soul. After deliverance has been effected, ask God to send angels to pick up the fragments of Alice's soul that were stolen away, to quicken them, and to put them back together in proper order with the rest of Alice's soul.

Fighting against Leviathan

There are many weapons given us by the Bible. When fighting with Leviathan, for instance, quote Job 41 and Isaiah 27:1–3.

Worker: Leviathan, I dry up your seas and your waters. I bind you up in the heavenlies. I put a thorn in your jaw, a hook in your nose, and a cord around your tongue.

I cut you off from Jezebel and Mind Control. You will not torment this woman. You piercing and crooked serpent, I command you to straighten out your crooked coils. You straighten out. You come out in Jesus' name. You come out of her heart, you piercing serpent (If the person grasps her heart and groans, do not be alarmed. Keep commanding the spirit to come out.)

The serpent will often move from the heart to the lower back, twine himself around the spine, or manifest on the upper shoulders and neck. The person will grasp her neck or lower back. Lay hands on the area, or if you are a man and the subject is a woman, have another woman lay hands on areas which men should not touch. Then you may lay hands on the other woman's hand. Continue on.

> **Worker:** You ugly serpent, I have been given all power to tread on serpents and scorpions and over all the power of the enemy and nothing shall by any means hurt me (Luke 10:19). I put you under my feet. (Sometimes, I stomp with my feet as I say that, and the spirit groans.)
>
> Listen to me, serpent, the Word of God says He will slay the dragon in the sea (Isaiah 27:1). I will break the heads of the dragons in the waters, the heads of Leviathan in pieces (Psalm 74:13–14). You come out in Jesus' name.

Keep repeating until the enemy comes out. Your words will be like arrows which bombard him, and the cumulative effect will drive him out. In particularly difficult cases, the session may last for up to an hour or more. In the beginning, I often fought for several hours. However, my sessions seldom go beyond thirty minutes now. If the person being prayed over or the workers are exhausted, it is often wise to stop and continue another day. If the workers are exhausted, other workers can be brought in, of course.

If Nothing Happens

Remember that deliverance always works. If results don't come, it is most likely one of two reasons: (1) Satan has a legal right somewhere; (2) God may not be the author of illness or demonic invasion, but He permits it in order to allow the afflicted to grow in Him. A person may refuse to grow and never receive healing or deliverance. For instance, God may want to clean you of unforgiveness for your father. If you refuse, the spirits do not leave, and the healing does not take place. I recall cases where long-time Christians suffered from illness that if not healed, eventually resulted in death. After many "failed" deliverances and healing prayers by countless people and by every visiting pastor or prophet, it is discovered that the "mature" Christian is living in sin or has not talked to her family for years because of bitterness or some other reason. God works everything together for the good of those who love Him. Often, however, Christians refuse to be dealt with. Many Christians appear to the world as holy and righteous but, on close inspection, have rebellion or unforgiveness in their hearts or refuse to give up hidden sin.

Chapter Thirteen

Leviathan

How deadly is the spirit of Pride. If there is one characteristic that separates Satan from God, it is pride. Every demon in hell is full of it. Adam and Eve disobeyed because of pride. Rebellion followed soon thereafter. Jesus, the image of the Father, is diametrically opposite. Philippians 2:8 says, *"And being found in fashion as a man, he humbled himself, and became obedient unto death, even the death of the cross."* Jesus said, *"I am among you as he that serveth"* (Luke 22:27). Pride versus humility is the leading difference between the two kingdoms.

Humility

There are many Scriptures in which Jesus instructs us to be meek and humble (Matt. 18:4; Luke 14:11; 18:14; John 13:14–17). The apostles also taught all Christians to be humble (1 Tim. 1:15–17; 1 Pet. 5:6).

Proverbs 18:12 points out the difference between pride and humility: *"Before destruction the heart of man is haughty, and before honour is humility."* In short, pride leads to destruction, but humility to honor. God promises to bring down the haughty. Isaiah 10:33 says, "*and the haughty shall be humbled.*" God desires and respects a humble heart.

> "*I* [God] *dwell in the high and holy place, with him also that is of a contrite and humble spirit, to revive the spirit of the humble, and to revive the heart of the contrite ones.* (Isa: 57:15)

There are many other Scriptures which teach God's people to be humble: 2 Chronicles 7:14; Job 22:29; Psalm 9:12; 10:17; Proverbs 16:19; Matthew 18:4; 23:12; James 4:6, 10; Luke 14:11; 18:14; Acts 20:19; 1 Peter 5:5.

Pride Will Bring Destruction

Isaiah 24:4 talks about the end-time destruction: "*The earth mourneth and fadeth away, the world languisheth and fadeth away, the haughty people of the earth do languish.*" The prophet once again talks about the end times and says, "*The lofty looks of man shall be humbled, and the haughtiness of men shall be bowed down, and the LORD alone shall be exalted in that day*" (Isa. 2:11). In Isaiah 5:15, he says, "*And the mean man shall be brought down, and the mighty man shall be humbled, and the eyes of the lofty shall be humbled.*"

Job 41

The Amplified Bible refers to Leviathan as the "*monarch over all the children of pride*" (Job 41:34).

Indeed, Leviathan's children are many. Leviathan stands out as one of the most powerful and wicked demons. God sometimes uses animals in the natural, such as serpents, scorpions, frogs, and goats to describe certain demons. When it comes to Leviathan, however, no animal on earth can describe it, so terrible is his countenance. God uses a mythical creature, a dragon, to describe Leviathan.

Like Jezebel, no one sees him. But God says, "*I will not conceal his parts, nor his power, nor his comely proportion*" (Job 41:12). His fierceness prevents any man from taming him. "*Who can discover the face of his garment? or who can come to him with his double bridle? Who can open the doors of his face? his teeth are terrible round about*" (vv. 13–14). The obvious answer is "Only God can do it." Can you tame pride? No man can.

> [Leviathan's] *scales are his pride, shut up together as with a close seal. One is so near to another, that no air can come between them. They are joined one to another, they stick together, that they cannot be sundered.*
>
> (Job 41:15–17)

Some deliverance writers claim that since the Bible likens the Holy Spirit to air or wind, the scales of Leviathan prevent Christians from receiving the things of God, including the gifts of the Holy Spirit, and smothers a born again Christian's spiritual growth. I can't argue with that.

> *By his neesings a light doth shine, and his eyes are like the eyelids of the morning. Out of his mouth go burning lamps, and sparks of fire*

*leap out. Out of his nostrils goeth smoke, as out
of a seething pot or caldron.* (Job 41:18–20)

It is said that Leviathan sits in the Holy Place,
counterfeits the furnishings, and blocks the entrance which leads into the Holy of Holies. He gives
a false peace and sense of well being by counterfeiting the gifts of the Holy Spirit—false revelations,
prophesies, words, visions, and dreams. His
"neesing" (sneezings) and mouth counterfeit the
golden lampstand with the seven lamps with its
"burning lamps and sparks of fire." In our Christian
walk, everything must be viewed through the light
of God. In the Holy Place, one could not see except
by the light of the seven lamps. Leviathan counterfeits and gives false light and, therefore, false understanding.

Spiritual pride leads Christians to cling to favorite doctrines and beliefs which cause them to become unteachable. They "camp" around certain
truths while God wants them to move on. They
stagnate in their understandings of the Word, seeing only through the false light of Leviathan. They
have vested interests in defending their beliefs, denominations, or churches. Leviathan has cut off the
true light.

Leviathan also counterfeits the table of showbread and gives a false word. Pride twists the Word
to support favorite doctrines and blocks all other
light on the Word. Many Christians accept counterfeit bread from heaven. Pride's scales are so tight
that they not only refuse to allow truth in, they refuse to allow false or limited doctrine out.

Pride often gives people mouth trouble. They love to criticize, judge, complain, find fault, ridicule, and challenge. Fire shoots out of their mouths. They love to argue, contend, and contest in order to show off their knowledge (or ignorance) of the Word. Pride can gossip through prayer: "Lord, please help brother Alfred who's beating up his wife and kids and running around with other women." Pride can convince people that they are chosen to be apostles and prophets because they received a fabulous prophecy ages ago, even though they remain immature. They become overbearing.

The fire and smoke from Leviathan's nostrils and mouth counterfeit the altar of incense. Instead of holy prayers and praises that please God, they produce unholy prayers and praises that stink. The Pharisee that says, "I thank you for not making me like that man over there" is worshipping out of Pride. Pride can stick its ugly head up and look around the church in the middle of praise and worship. He can open his mouth and speak words of pride in the middle of intercessory prayer.

Verse 31 mentions a seething pot or caldron: *"He maketh the deep to boil like a pot; he maketh the sea like a pot of ointment."* We liken the deep to that part of man where the inner man dwells—the innermost part of man. Leviathan often makes the deep boil like a pot of ointment. He stirs up your emotions and will. Pride seethes deep within. People with Leviathan act calm and peaceful in church. However, as soon as they are on the way home, Leviathan acts up, and they soon start screaming and boiling over—yelling at the spouse and children.

Restlessness, sleeplessness, and turmoil deep inside someone often indicate the presence of Leviathan.

> *In his neck remaineth strength, and sorrow is turned into joy before him. The flakes of his flesh are joined together: they are firm in themselves; they cannot be moved. His heart is as firm as a stone; yea, as hard as a piece of the nether millstone.* (Job 41:22–24)

People yielding to the Leviathan spirit become stiff-necked. They look neither to the right nor left because they have a one-track mind. You cannot change them. They are like concrete—all mixed up and thoroughly set in their ways. Their hearts become hard. The *"nether millstone"* refers to the bottom stone of the gristmill upon which ancient millers ground grain. Millers form the nether millstone out of the hardest rock available. God called the Hebrew nation hardhearted and stiff-necked. (See Exodus 32:9 and Ezekiel 3:7.) This same description applies to people who have the Leviathan spirit. Daniel 5:20 says of King Nebuchadnezzar: *"his heart was lifted up, and his mind hardened in pride."*

The flakes of his flesh join so tightly together that they cannot be moved. If the flakes or scales on a serpent cannot be moved, the serpent itself cannot be moved. People with Pride cannot be moved and, therefore, are unable to grow. They cling to ideas and doctrines that prevent personal growth. It would be admitting that they were wrong, and Pride never allows one to be wrong.

More Than Pride

Leviathan represents more than simple pride. Pride forms the very basis of sin. All types of disobedience and rebellion find their roots in pride. Jesus, the very image of the Father, stood for humility. Jesus says, "I am meek and humble." Without humility, love and submission become only hollow words. Pride prevents obedience to God.

Pride works in many subtle ways within the body of Christ. It gives a false feeling of peace and well-being. You may feel growth, peace, and comfort, but Leviathan gives false gifts and false worship. Leviathan wraps or coils itself around your heart, and you feel that everything is great. Gradually, your prayers become dry, your worship dead, and your praise hardly reaches the ceiling. It's difficult to receive a word from God, and sometimes you wonder whether God is angry and not talking to you anymore. If you find yourself in that situation, Leviathan may be at work.

Over the Church

Leviathan flops on the church like a wet blanket that smothers. You can hardly breathe because of the oppression. His air-tight scales cut off the Holy Spirit. One of Leviathan's main jobs is to stop deliverance ministries. He stifles and kills the anointing. You can pray deliverance over people and nothing happens. People don't feel like ministering deliverance, and others don't feel like they need any deliverance. The body of Christ languishes in spiritual kindergarten today largely due to Leviathan's handiwork.

Some people discern a cover over the church. Others experience a hazy smoke that makes breathing difficult. Leviathan counterfeits the glory of God. The fruit of the Spirit shrivels up. Not only deliverance, but healings and other gifts of the Holy Spirit choke and sputter. If you experience sleepiness in service, difficulty in reading the Bible, daily devotions, or in praying, whether in church or in private, Leviathan may be at work.

Manifestations

A Slug

Sometimes Leviathan is spiritually discerned as a black slug or snail. He puts people in prison, and there is no liberty. You see others moving in the Holy Spirit and yearn to be like them. They seem to be going at fifty miles per hour while you move at five with difficulty.

Leviathan is the one that rules over the Laodicean church. He makes believers think that good works and wealth equal holiness, and that the world admires them. They are complacent because everyone recognizes his good works and wealth.

This ugly spirit also brings dejection, mental oppression, and many other emotional problems. Stopping revivals and other forms of spiritual growth comprises one of its major tasks. Prayer meetings soon lose the zeal and enthusiasm they originally had when Leviathan is at work.

Pride brings Rebellion. "Why should we listen to the pastor? After all, he's no better than we are. We don't have to submit to him, he has to submit to us. Without us, he would be without a job." Where Pride is, Rebellion, Discord, and Sedition are sure to be found. Pride is what tells people that God wants them to go around to different churches to set the pastors right. Yet, these same individuals never submit to any one.

A Corkscrew

Leviathan, the crooked serpent, reminds us of a corkscrew. It's hard to pull a crooked nail or corkscrew out of something. Likewise, Leviathan's crookedness makes it difficult to extract him. The Scriptures also describe him as a piercing serpent.

> *In that day the LORD with his sore and great and strong sword shall punish leviathan the piercing serpent, even leviathan that crooked serpent; and he shall slay the dragon that is in the sea.* (Isa. 27:1)

Multiple Heads

Leviathan has multiple heads. Leviathan particularly hates Psalm 74:13–14 which says,

> *Thou didst divide the sea by thy strength: thou brakest the heads of the dragons in the waters. Thou brakest the heads of leviathan in pieces, and gavest him to be meat to the people inhabiting the wilderness.*

He also hates the following Scripture:

In that day the LORD with his sore and great and strong sword shall punish leviathan the piercing serpent, even leviathan that crooked serpent; and he shall slay the dragon that is in the sea. (Isa. 27:1)

The Bible says he has heads but not how many. We have found that Leviathan in one person may have different or more heads as compared to the same spirit in another person. For instance, one person may possess Pride of Body, Sex, the World, or Riches, and another person may yield to Spiritual Pride in singing or in prophesying. In that sense, the exact number of heads seems immaterial.

God Can Handle It

It is impossible for you and me to handle Leviathan by ourselves in the flesh, but with the Holy Spirit, we can cast Leviathan out using Job 41. Verses 1 and 2 are definitely warfare Scriptures. God is saying, "You cannot, but I can." In verse 11, He says, *"Who hath prevented me, that I should repay him? whatsoever is under the whole heaven is mine."*

While Jeremiah 50 and 51 refer specifically to Babylon the Great, note that the Bible names Pride as one of Babylon's helpers. As mentioned earlier, when discussing Jezebel in Nahum 3:9, the Word of God says this about Babylon: *"Ethiopia and Egypt were her strength, and it was infinite; Put and Lubim were thy helpers."* Ethiopia was a close ally of

Egypt. We know that city as a major port of commerce which dealt heavily in gold, silver, and other riches of the world. The Bible describes Egypt as a city known for her pomp and pride of power. In fact, the Pharaoh is spoken of in almost identical terms as with Leviathan (Job 41:1–2).

> *Speak, and say, Thus saith the Lord GOD;*
> *Behold, I am against thee, Pharaoh king of*
> *Egypt, the great dragon that lieth in the midst*
> *of his rivers, which hath said, My river is*
> *mine own, and I have made it for myself. But*
> *I will put hooks in thy jaws, and I will cause*
> *the fish of thy rivers to stick unto thy scales,*
> *and I will bring thee up out of the midst of thy*
> *rivers, and all the fish of thy rivers shall stick*
> *unto thy scales.*   (Ezekiel 29:3–4)

God specifically calls the Pharaoh of Egypt a dragon. He also talks about putting hooks into Pharaoh's jaw which is identical to the language found in Job 41:1.

Deliverance

Leviathan customarily comes down the family line as a curse. You need to break that curse by the blood of our Lord Jesus. Use Galatians 3:13, and ask God to break the curses backwards ten generations on each side of the family.

Like other strongmen, Leviathan uses many other spirits to cover specific areas. The person needs to repent for his or her yielding to the spirits listed below. In the area of mass deliverance, we ask the people to stand and verbally confess any sin of involvement and ask for forgiveness as we call out the names of various spirits. The list below can be added to and does not represent the sum total of all the spirits that Leviathan uses. The children of Pride are:

Pride of Body	Swearing	Backbiting
Pride of Intellect	Criticism	Arrogance
Pride of Sexual Power	Conceitedness	Spiritual Pride
Pride of Worldly Things	Selfishness	False Humility
Pride of Power	Greed	Boasting
Pride of Money	Possessions	Challenging
Idolatry/Worship of Self	Bragging	Arguing
Hard-Heartedness	Lying	Contention
Prideful Looks	Exaggeration	Disputing
Lawyer/Contesting	Slumber	Questioning
Vain Imaginations	Slothfulness	Cheating
Impatience	Laziness	Rebellion
Disobedience	Idleness	Destruction
Sauciness	Impurity	Snares
Mincing Steps	Bullying	Cords
Let-Others-Do-It	Disrespect	Nets
Judgmentalism	Lawlessness	Traps
Self-Righteousness	Scorner	Noose
Complaining	Strife	Perverseness
Looking Down	Vanity	Error
Putting Down	Corruption	False Prosperity
Gossiping	Oppression	Cheating
Laughing at Others	Blasphemy	Cursing
Misfortune	Slander	Deception
Prince Charming	Mocking	Dead Works
Cinderella	Shame	False Prophecy
False Compassion	Proud Wrath	False Doctrines
Vivid Imagination	Jealousy	Unfruitfulness
Haughtiness	Unforgiveness	Deep Hurt
Rejection of Others	Superiority	Envy
Accusation of Others	Drunkenness	Self-Pity
Disrespect for Authority	Condemnation	Violence

Confrontation	Suspicion	Depression
Pride of Life	Reproach	Suicide
Pride of the World	Discredit	Guilt
Lust of Flesh	Wickedness	Perfection
Lust of the Eyes	Gluttony	Unfairness
Deception	Loftiness	Fantasy
Ignorance	Confusion	Anger
Unteachableness	Hatred	Control
Deceitfulness	Intolerance	Possessiveness
Cunning	High Looks	Frustration
Self-Seduction	Foolishness	Guile
Self-Will	Retaliation	Resentment

As in every other area of deliverance, repentance is the key. Without repentance, there is no forgiveness. Without forgiveness, the sin continues. Where sin exists, demons own the right to torment.

You need to bind up Leviathan in the heavenlies as a ruling spirit and cut off all cords between Leviathan and any spirits in the person.

Since Leviathan lives in the sea, dry up its waters. Quote Jeremiah 50:38 and Jeremiah 51:36: "*A drought is upon her waters; and they shall be dried up*" and "*I will dry up her sea, and make her springs dry.*" Quote also Luke 10:19: "Spirit, listen to what the Lord Jesus said to me and all believers: '*Behold, I give unto you power to tread on serpents and scorpions, and over all the power of the enemy: and nothing shall by any means hurt you.*' "I put you under my feet and I stomp on your heads."

I commonly use the following sequence or a similar pattern:

In the name of Jesus and by the power of His blood, I put a hook in your jaw and a

cord around your tongue. I bore your jaw
through with a thorn, in Jesus' name.

Leviathan often manifests itself by giving pain
and stiffness in the area of the neck and shoulders
to the person being delivered. The spirit of Rejection
also does this and small wonder, since the spirit of
Pride plays a major role in rejection. The person will
grasp his neck and arch his back. Sometimes, the
spirit of Pride manifests by rippling up the person's
spinal column. At other times, he coils around the
heart, and the person will hold his chest in pain.
Once the spirit manifests, you need to continue to
pound it with Scriptures. Always obey the Holy
Spirit in spiritual warfare.

If the demon refuses to leave within ten to fifteen minutes, it probably has a legal right. The person most likely needs to confess an area of sin or
unforgiveness, and then repent. The rule remains
inviolate.

Remember, Leviathan possesses more than one
head. You need to go after all heads. Each one represents a formidable and deep area of pride, sometimes covered up by our own cunning ability to hide
our conceit and deviousness from ourselves as well
as others. False Humility covers up Pride until the
right circumstances expose our true condition. Anyone can act humble when confronted by people
above his station in life, but the same person will
look down on people he considers below his level. A
street beggar may bow to the businessman in his
Cadillac, but he will kick the fellow beggar next to
him.

Having by faith bound up Leviathan in the heavenlies, and cutting off all cords, take authority over individual spirits of Leviathan as listed above. As the Holy Spirit leads, go after individual spirits that make up the children of Pride.

Remember, Pride represents the underlying foundation for all sin. Our battle with Pride is life-long. It prevents Christians from entering into the deepest realms of the Spirit. It deceives us into thinking that we are profitable servants of God because we have zeal, enthusiasm, works, and all the characteristics of a good servant of God. The whole time however, we are doing things for ourselves, to make us look good in the eyes of others. It may be a desire for recognition, or for the simple reason that such actions are part of our religion and doctrine. I, me, and mine are the motivation for our actions. If what you do has a basis other than your love for God or for your neighbor, chances are that it is steeped in pride.

Chapter Fourteen

The Spirit of Antichrist

Antichrist is a worldwide power as well as a ruling spirit. It is found both inside and outside the church. It is the power that opposes God's kingdom. The prefix "anti" implies something is against to or opposite from something else. It has been around for a long time, perhaps since the Garden of Eden. It is the spirit of a religion that honors the flesh, part of the Babylonian system that covers the earth today.

There will be an individual called the Antichrist who will personify everything that is against Christ. In the end times, this evil antichrist power will reach its climax in activity and evil.

The Spirit of the World

The Antichrist spirit is of the world and speaks about things of the world. People yielding to that spirit respond to the world, know the world, approve of the world, delve into the world, and appreciate the things of the world, and the world responds to them. They love the world and the world loves and hears them. As much as the world loves unbelievers, it hates the followers of Jesus Christ. Jesus said that *"the world hath hated them, because they are not of the world, even as I am not of the world"* (John 17:14).

Politics, government, business, banking, military, music, sports, medicine, law, entertainment, movies, TV, education, religion, and many other activities are antichrist in nature. All that is in the world and opposes God belongs to Antichrist. All that the world stands for, which denies the Father and the Son, is Antichrist. Many Christians never really left the world, and they leave the church to go back into worldly pursuits. That is how you know that they are not true Christians. They serve the spirit of Antichrist and Mammon.

Anytime you touch the world, you touch Satan's kingdom. Christ's kingdom is not of this world. Churches are beachheads of Christ's kingdom dwelling in Satan's kingdom, strangers in a foreign land. We dwell in Satan's domain, but we remain separate and distinct. We came out of the world and walked into God's Kingdom. Satan hates Christians because they stand out as beacons in the midst of his dark domain. Satan would love to have us fall to the lusts of this world, the substitute system that opposes God's sovereignty.

Satan sets many traps to ensnare us with the cares of this world by the thorns and thistles of debt, greed, power, material possessions, luxuries, broken relationships, money, worldly ambitions, and sexual lust. He set the world up so that the pulls affect each Christian.

In Colossians 4:14, Paul writes *"Luke, the beloved physician, and Demas, greet you."* In Philemon 24, Paul once again mentions Demas, part of *"my fellowlabourers."* In 2 Timothy 4:10, Paul makes this sad report, *"For Demas hath forsaken me, having loved this present world, and is departed unto Thessalonica"* So you see, the pulls of the world ensnared and convinced Demas to leave the ministry, and perhaps the faith. The spirit of Antichrist continues to pull many Christians back into the world, even some who have seen the power of God and worked faithfully for years.

Citizens of a Foreign Land

We live in the world and must use it, but we must not be ensnared by it. Jesus came eating and drinking. He used the things of the world, but He never became ensnared by them. We live by the Spirit and can take or leave the world. We possess things, but when things start to possess us, that's when the spirit of Antichrist controls us. We touch the world, but we learn to detach ourselves. We remain citizens in a foreign land. Paul said,

> But this I say, brethren, the time is short: it remaineth, that both they that have wives be as though they have none; and they that weep, as though they wept not; and they that rejoice, as though they rejoiced not; and they that buy,

as though they possessed not; and they that use
this world, as not abusing it: for the fashion of
this world passeth away.   (1 Cor. 7:29–31)

Paul says we may have wives, but we should not favor wives over the things of God, or the things of the world over the things of the Spirit. We obey God before our wives and we do the things of God, not the things of the world, in order to please our wives. Our love for our wives is secondary to our love for God.

We weep and yet we can let it go because we put the things of God above worldly possessions and riches. If we lose possessions and riches we weep not, although the rest of the world would weep for the loss. We rejoice over gain, and yet we rejoice not. We know that the things of the world become transitory and worthless in the heavenly realm. We can weep or rejoice like the rest of the world, and yet it affects us not at all, for our joy rests in the Lord, not in the things of the world. We look like citizens of the world and can laugh and weep, but we come from another kingdom. We live in the world, and yet we live outside of the world. (Read Watchman Nee's wonderful book entitled *Love Not the World*.)

We need to be aware not only of the physical world, but of the demonic power behind it. Behind everything in the world that is not of God hides a demonic power—the Antichrist spirit. Every time we touch the things of the world, we touch the demonic power behind the world. We need to be very careful when we touch the things of the world. They can become Satan's snare, the snare of the fowler (Ps. 91:3).

Every time you watch sports or commercials promoting various beauty aids and self-help products, you touch part of the demonic realm that controls the world. Every time you watch sexy ads, beauty contests, or sexually arousing programs, you're touching the demonic power of the world. Every time you get involved in some business deal, political activity, or some organization outside of the church, you're touching the demonic realm—the Antichrist spirit.

The activities of the world do not honor or promote God's kingdom. Almost everything outside of the church promotes the coming of the Antichrist. The industries of entertainment, banking, military, medicine, law, commerce, sports, business, and even some religions (pseudo Christian churches included), promote and prepare for the coming of Antichrist. The world's activities lead inexorably to the Antichrist in the end times. One can definitely observe opposition to Christ in each of these areas and all other areas of life that are not of God.

For instance, the entertainment industry pushes sex, violence, and rebellion. It promotes satanic music and movies. Even children's cartoons push demonic ideas. The banking industry slowly, but surely, contributes to setting up a one world economic system featuring a cashless society, debit cards (credit cards), and the sign of the beast. The global military gears itself up for world conflict and destruction, and will play a major role in suppressing and persecuting Christians in the end times. Medicine promotes abortion and the idea that only the laws of nature and evolution exist, not God. The legal profession with its worldliness, greed, and desire for power represents ungodliness. The government inexorably creates laws that push the nation away from God. It prohibits prayer in schools while allowing meditation and visualization under the guise of self-improvement. The educational system teaches witchcraft and ungodliness. Commerce and business motivate themselves towards greed, world control, and personal gain. They accept any product, so long as it makes money, including pornography, liquor, and drugs. The political arena endorses greed for power, money, fame, and a one-world government. Evil permeates every segment of society, setting the stage for the Antichrist. Neither mankind nor the world has changed a whit over the centuries. Man just invented more ingenious methods of committing sin.

Babylon the Great

The entire world makes up the Babylonian religion and the system created by Satan in opposition to God. All that exists in the world which is not of God falls under the control and evil influence of Babylon, Satan's empire. You cannot walk between the two. Either you serve God or you serve Mammon. *"Come out of her, my people, that ye be not partakers of her sins, and that ye receive not of her plagues"* (Rev. 18:4).

Many Christian writers claim the beast that rises from the sea in Revelation 13:1 represents the

Antichrist. Verse 7 says, "*And it was given unto him to make war with the saints, and to overcome them: and power was given him over all kindreds, and tongues, and nations.*" While we busy ourselves looking for an individual Antichrist, the spirits of Antichrist already work in our churches to overcome the saints. Many are still fornicating in Babylon.

Christians need to be very careful when they walk in this world. Hidden traps wait to ensnare us everywhere. I've heard Christians claim that the reason they get involved in questionable promotions and business transactions is because God wants them to have a ministry of giving. In ninety percent of the cases, that is pure baloney. Most of them result in failure anyway, and such Christians always seem to be in financial trouble. If God wants to give them a ministry of giving, He will provide the success that generates the funds while keeping their integrity intact

Many Christians dip into the world through sex. They compromise with the world and enjoy the fruits of Babylon. They sneak into porno theaters and read racy magazines while proclaiming their liberty in the Holy Spirit and their ability to control their desires. Sooner or later they fall into outright sexual sin.

You can't walk the fence. You will topple into the world's side sooner or later. You must come out of Babylon away from its things that entice and entrap. Even a little opening can give Satan entry into your life. On the other hand, coming out of Babylon does not mean that you must become Amish or a recluse. Draw closer to God and forsake the things of the world that pull you away.

Antichrist represents far more than a different Jesus, it is a worldwide spiritual power and system which entraps. The antichrist is a veritable Egypt that sucks people back into sin. How often did the Hebrews want to go back into captivity and bondage after God took them out of Egypt? The flesh makes bondage look appealing at times.

The spirits of Antichrist manifest today in the lives of Christians who continue to covet the things of the world. They cannot give up smoking or drinking. They still love their expensive cars, clothing, and food. The prosperity message is a fruit of the Antichrist spirit. It creates covetousness and pride. A backsliding Christian may be a victim of the spirit of Antichrist. God wants His people to prosper, but not by ways of the world. David and Solomon prospered and then fell into sin through worldly things.

A System of Lies

In the church, the spirit manifests through constant deception and the distortion of doctrine. Seducing spirits entice groups into following leaders who seem to be charismatic and natural. This spirit works to twist the true gospel of the kingdom into a worldly religion of prosperity and good works. Churches under the influence of this spirit love ceremonies, rituals, and good works. You can find ample good works, but little spiritual growth and understanding. They do not believe in tongues, the

work or gifts of the Holy Spirit, miracles, or supernatural things. They base their religion on logic and
sometimes science. The Antichrist spirit works with
things of the world and will bend the Word of God to
fit the world and the flesh. That is why Paul spoke
so plainly in Romans, chapter eight about walking
in the spirit. The flesh desires the things of the
world; the spirit desires the things of God. "*For as
many as are led by the Spirit of God, they are the
sons of God*" (v. 14).

The Bible mentions the spirit of Antichrist by
name in only four verses:

> *Little children, it is the last time: and as ye
> have heard that antichrist shall come, even
> now are there many antichrists; whereby we
> know that it is the last time. They went out
> from us, but they were not of us; for if they
> had been of us, they would no doubt have con-
> tinued with us: but they went out, that they
> might be made manifest that they were not all
> of us.* (1 John 2:18–19)

> *Who is a liar but he that denieth that Jesus is
> the Christ? He is antichrist, that denieth the
> Father and the Son.* (1 John 2:22)

> *And every spirit that confesseth not that Jesus
> Christ is come in the flesh is not of God: and
> this is that spirit of antichrist, whereof ye
> have heard that it should come; and even now
> already is it in the world.* (1 John 4:3)

> *For many deceivers are entered into the world,
> who confess not that Jesus Christ is come in*

the flesh. This is a deceiver and an antichrist.
(2 John 1:7)

John makes a number of interesting statements. Verse eighteen of chapter two indicates that as the end times approach, the Antichrist spirit becomes more powerful and numerous. It operates from within the church, causing people to leave and start their own cult or denomination or simply fall away. Since over 261 Protestant denominations exist in America today, the fruits are obvious. The peak activity of Antichrist will result in the falling away mentioned in the Bible.

Let no man deceive you by any means: for that
day shall not come, except there come a falling
away first, and that man of sin be revealed,
the son of perdition.   (2 Thess. 2:3)

Most deliverance workers come across this spirit sparingly and know very little about it. This spirit is mentioned as the first Beast by the apostle John in the book of Revelation chapter thirteen. There apparently will be an Antichrist which will appear as an individual man or beast. But there are also many Antichrist spirits already at work in the world to set the stage for the coming of the individual Antichrist. As an end-time spirit, Antichrist increases in power with time.

Over the centuries, we can observe a constant falling away of Christians, even beginning with Paul's time. In the end times, however, a massive falling away will take place. Many Christians will return to the world or become entrapped by false teachings.

A Different Jesus

The prefix "anti" means "instead of" and therefore, we can see that the spirit of Antichrist brings a different christ from the one found in God's Word. It is a deception that creates a false Jesus. One need not look far to find a "different" Jesus.

The Jehovah Witnesses claim that Jesus was created by God, thus denying His deity and His role in the Godhead (1 John 2:22). The Mormons say that Jesus is the brother of Satan. Others claim that Jesus is a Filipino living secretly in Manila. Some claim He is a Korean by the name of Moon. New Agers say that Jesus is an ascended master, an avatar, like the enlightened gurus of old. New Agers, Hindus, and Buddhists claim that we are all christs and have the Christ light in us.

New Agers also claim that the end of the world will reveal seven ascended masters, including Jesus, but Jesus is only one of seven. They claim Kathumi, the reincarnation of Saint Francis, is the highest of the masters. The others include a Tibetan master, a Buddha, a Hindu guru, a Indian sorcerer, and a shaman. What Jesus sits on the throne in your heart?

The Gateway for Antichrist

The opening for the spirit of Antichrist is self. Rees Howells once said, "The problem is not sin, it is self" (Grubb 40). Self in the church represents rebellion against authority, pride, stubbornness, and lack of submission. The desire of self on the throne will lead you back to the world.

Deliverance from Antichrist

Repentance and a genuine desire to serve God set the stage for deliverance from the spirit of Antichrist. This spirit works in conjunction with other ruling spirits such as Jezebel, Pride, and Mind Control. You need to bind up those strongmen and cut off the cords between the strongmen in the heavenlies and those in the person.

Antichrist comes out of the sea. Dry up his waters. Proceed to cast him out using the same techniques as with other spirits. Let the Holy Spirit lead you. Antichrist works with the following spirits:

Greed	Fleshiness	Blasphemy
Covetousness	Idolatry	Disobedience
Gambling	Pride	Rebellion
Desire for Wealth,	Self-Glory	Unbelief
Power, Sexual	Lawlessness	Doubt
Recognition,	Lack of Respect	Vanity
and Fame	Worldliness	Reasonings
Overindulgence in	Witchcraft	Logic
Entertainment,	False Doctrines	Science
Alcohol, Drugs,	Strange Religions	Distrust
Sex, and Food		

Chapter Fifteen

The Spirit of Mind Control

S atan wants to control the minds of all the inhabitants of the world in order to force them to worship him. God, on the other hand, gives us liberty to love and serve Him.

As we pointed out in Ezekiel 13:18–21, Witchcraft steals the souls of men and women. The soul contains the intellect, emotions, and will. I recall a story in which policemen invaded the home of a witch. They found hundreds of empty jars, each with a label containing someone's name. A knowledgeable officer recognized those jars as containing the souls of many individuals who had been "bewitched" by the coven.

A person who is under the power of the Witchcraft Mind Control spirit finds himself subject to uncontrollable urges and thoughts. Certain emotions and feelings arise unexpectedly. Despondency and mood swings mark his personality. Memories of the past haunt him and certain addictions increase, including drugs, alcohol, and masturbation. He feels compelled to do certain things or to act in certain ways. Often, anger and bitterness emerge unexpectedly and just as quickly subside.

Deception

Satan's most powerful weapon is deception. Second Thessalonians 2:3 says, "*Let no man deceive you by any means: for that day shall not come, except there come a falling away first, and that man of sin be revealed, the son of perdition.*" In the end times, many saints will fall away from the faith because of deception. Jesus Himself warns of deception (Matt. 24:12, 24). Revelation 13:14 says that Satan's beast will deceive the whole world (except the mature in God) into worshipping him.

Deceived people do not know that they are deceived. They have accepted lies as truth. They absolutely believe the lies that the enemy has fed them. Their minds are set and controlled by Satan, the father of lies (John 8:44).

Planting Lies

Once you believe in a lie, you are trapped. There are many ways to introduce lies into your mind, most of them so clever and insidious that you are never conscious of them. Do not be fooled: they run your life.

Satan does not need to put everybody in a trance before he can place suggestions in the mind. All he needs is an opportunity, and just about all of us are susceptible. The opportunity usually comes when a traumatic incident takes place, such as physical accidents, personal losses, and times of extreme embarrassment, fear, stress, or rejection. It can happen when a simple suggestion or lie is accepted at that time.

Let's look at three examples from real-life experiences:

Case One:

Bertha just broke up with her boyfriend. The week before, her boyfriend informed Bertha that he was falling in love with her. Suddenly, Bertha could not stand him. She told him that she hated him and did not want to see him ever again. The boyfriend is totally perplexed. Bertha is unhappy. Upon my persistent questioning, Bertha recalls that at age ten, she was sitting in her bedroom with her nine year old sister. Unknown to Bertha, her sister had leukemia and, therefore, only a few months to live. Her parents had not told Bertha because they felt that she was too young. The parents quite naturally spoiled Bertha's sister. In the bedroom, Bertha told her sister that she hated her and wished she were dead. Two months later, the sister died.

Bertha had made a decision never to let anyone get close to her because he would learn the awful secret that she was a murderer. She believed she did not deserve happiness, and she feared that anyone who got close to her would die. Satan had come in with a lie, and Bertha had agreed with it and accepted it as truth.

Bertha later learned of the leukemia, but it was too late. She had already agreed with Satan's cruel lie. Bertha unconsciously lived her life in agreement with it. Within a few years, she had broken up with seven different boyfriends. Bertha was a stunning redhead with green eyes that men found very attractive, but she had a phobia.

We renounced the lie and asked Jesus to heal her memories. Bertha's life changed.

Case Two:

Dan was almost stone deaf. He had worn a hearing aid since the age of fifteen. Deafness had set in around age twelve. During a deep discussion about his problem, he suddenly recalled an incident when his parents were yelling at each other. He distinctly remembered his father screaming at Dan's mother, "You're a whore, you're a whore." Dan covered his ears and said to himself, "I don't want to hear that, I don't want to hear that." Soon thereafter, Dan started going deaf. He never related the deafness to the incident and forgot about it until he was fifty-five years old. Dan then renounced the suggestion.

Exactly one week later, Dan returned. He now has no hearing aid and can hear perfectly.

Case Three:

Janice has almost completed the proceedings of a bad divorce. She hated her husband who ran off with a woman he met on his bowling team. Janice denies any responsibility for it. During a discussion on the matter, however, Janice remembered something about fourth grade. She did all of her homework at school, and at home her neighbor and best friend copied it. At the end of the school year, the best friend won the prize for having the neatest homework. In high school, another best friend stole Janice's boyfriend.

I asked Janice what she got out of it. Janice replied, "Nothing, all I know is you can't trust anybody who tries to get close to you." Janice suddenly broke down in loud crying.

Janice remembered that her husband was always nice when they first got married, but he would stick around her too much which she didn't like. He would complain that whenever he tried to get close to her, she grew cold. One day, Janice got tired of her husband hanging around (he loved to stay around the house fixing things and watching TV) so she told him to go join something like a bowling team. Her husband met his girlfriend on the bowling team. Of course, the girlfriend could not imagine why Janice threw such a sweet man away.

Negative and false decisions bought by people can prevent them from receiving salvation, growing in the Lord, or from receiving many things that God has set before them. Many Christians want deliverance or healing and cannot attain it because subconsciously they have agreed with one of Satan's lies. Demons will not leave if you want them to stay. If you have agreed that it is good to have anger so people will not push you around, the anger demons will not go.

Healing Memories

Inner healing and healing of memories include exposing lies and breaking agreements with lies. Most counselors, however, fail to recognize the enemy's lies and concentrate more on the effects of the lie. Failure to wipe out the lie, however, keeps the door open for future mind control. If you only cut off the leaves and branches, with the roots still intact, the tree will grow again.

You need to have the person recognize and acknowledge the lie that they agreed with when the traumatic incident occurred. Once they realize what the lie is, they need to use the Word of Truth to completely obliterate the lie. Lies are very powerful, but the truth will set you free (John 8:32). We seldom realize how much of our minds Satan has placed in bondage with his awful lies. James 1:21 says, *"receive with meekness the engrafted word, which is able to save your souls."*

I recommend the following sequence or something similar to it:

Worker: Bertha, do you now realize that the devil gave you a lie and that you are not a murderer?

Bertha: Yes.

Worker: Let me lead you through a prayer.

Bertha: I renounce the lie of Satan. I am not a murderer, I am loved by God. The Bible says that nothing can separate me from the love of God. Jesus knew me by name before He laid the foundations of the world.

Jesus said that He would never leave me

nor forsake me. He loves me, and I am worthy to be loved and to love in return. Jesus said that He would be with me always. I love Him and forgive myself for believing the lie of the devil.

Hypnotism

Another area of mind control involves hypnotism. Hypnotism opens the mind to demonic control. There are many methods used to establish hypnotic control. Some use devices, some use chants, and others use drugs, but the result is the same—opening the door to demonic invasion through suggestion. Entire nations have been mass hypnotized. Nazi Germany is a good example. In the end times, Satan will mass hypnotize entire nations and populations and convince them to kill all Christians. Have no doubt, Mind Control is a worldwide power.

A Giant Squid

The spirit of Mind Control is often seen as a giant squid with ten tentacles that stick into brains or cover heads (Worley 20–22). It is sometimes seen as a brown cylinder or dark brown bands that cover your body or head.

After praying one night over the spirit of mind control, God gave me the following vision:

I found myself floating a few hundred feet above a park-like clearing. I saw a grassy area surrounded by trees. In the center of the clearing, someone held a large bunch of balloons with varied colors. In the second scene, I saw a man with a wide, dark brown band around his head and around his body. The bands appeared almost black in color and looked like the metal bands that hold wooden barrels together. Suddenly something cut or broke the bands, and they fell off. The man smiled. Immediately, I found myself above the park again. Then, I saw the balloons floating freely up towards and beyond me. It seemed as if the person holding the balloons had let them go. They floated into the heavens.

The very next day I sat in church discussing the spirit of mind control. The assistant pastor shared that he had received a vision the night before in which he found himself bound up with dark brown bands around his head and body. We went after the spirit of Mind Control that night, and a number of people received deliverance from that spirit.

In Job 38:31, God says, "*Canst thou bind the sweet influences of Pleiades, or loose the bands of Orion?*" The spirit of Orion is in the family of spirits of Pride. In astronomy, seven stars make up the constellation Orion. Greek legend calls Orion "the mighty hunter." He stands with a club in one hand and a lion skin on his belt. He faces Taurus the bull in the sky. According to Greek legend, his lover Diana accidentally killed him when Diana's brother, who hated Orion, challenged Diana to shoot an arrow and hit a floating object in the lake. The floating object happened to be Orion's head, which Diana did not realize. Her arrow struck and killed him. In her remorse, Diana placed Orion in the heavens where he achieved immortality.

Door Openers

There are different things that can open the door for the spirit of Mind Control. Fear is one of them. Fear colors the way you think. Everything in the mind is slanted to reach a result pre-arranged by fear. A good example is the Hebrew nation as she came out of Egypt. No matter how many miracles the people saw God do, they could not shake the spirit of Fear. Fear caused them to forget what God had shown them, and to disobey. When the twelve spies were sent by Joshua to spy out the land, they saw wonderful things, but they also saw giants. All they focused on were the giants, so they forgot about the milk and honey. That night, they cried and wept. The spirit of Fear had overcome their minds.

Only two men were not afraid—Caleb and Joshua (Num. 14:6). In verse twenty-four, God said, *"But my servant Caleb, because he had another spirit with him, and hath followed me fully."* The spirit of Fear was not in Caleb, so Caleb was of a different mind.

Satan sometimes uses desire and even good intentions. In Genesis 3:5, the serpent lied to Eve and gave her a wonderful picture of how she would be as a god, knowing good and evil. It sounded so good that it changed her vision. Verse six says,

And when the woman saw that the tree was good for food, and that it was pleasant to the

eyes, and a tree to be desired to make one wise,
she took of the fruit thereof.   (Gen. 3:6)

The lie even changed Eve's sight. Suddenly, she had a different mind. Mankind, after almost 6,000 years, still seeks godhood. Hinduism, Buddhism, Shintoism, Taoism, New Age, and many other worldwide religions claim that man is, or can become, God.

Other things can change and control your mind, like hatred, bitterness, and unforgiveness. Your best friend becomes a hated enemy once he hurts you. You entire mental outlook can change overnight.

Addiction to drugs is a form of mind control. So is gluttony. Somewhere, fear, pride, or a lie can come in and control your mind. Satan has captured the minds of many. Schizophrenia and other mental diseases are on the rise. These victims no longer have control over their own thinking processes. They have bought the suggestions of the enemy and can no longer resist his evil schemes.

Meditation

Meditation represents one of the most insidious techniques ever devised by Satan. Millions of people around the world blank out their minds and bring their bodies into passivity through meditation. Hindus, Buddhists, Taoists, Shintoists, New Agers, and many other cults promote meditation. Satan even duped our schools into dumping prayer in favor of adopting meditation and chanting, all under the guise of relaxation techniques, mental awareness, and other lies. Transcendental meditation, Beta level techniques, and other disciplines come out of the very pit of hell. They creep into our churches under a guise of inner healing, Jesus chanting, "waiting," or "tarrying" meetings. God sometimes desires that we tarry in order to hear His voice. However, these tarrying meetings involve more than that. Many concentrate on seeing Jesus and looking into His eyes or focusing on Him, all while repeating "Jesus, Jesus."

A very interesting book is Jessie Penn-Lewis's publication *War On The Saints*. In her book, Mrs. Penn-Lewis exposes Satan's attacks on the minds and bodies of men and women by convincing them to "wait" on God by creating a passive mind and body. We notice many schizophrenic patients "zoning out" even when they are not on drugs. These victims need to retake their minds by forcing themselves to concentrate on whatever they are doing. Once they adopt the habit of going passive, they are easily swayed by voices and ideas passed to them by Satan. "The voices told me to do it," they claim. These victims begin to dress weirdly and assume peculiar acts of behavior that detract from their testimonies of God. Sometimes they don uniforms as a group and use strange slogans and militaristic attitudes. They become outcasts from the body and neutralized by demonic powers. Many cults fall into this category.

Satan also attempts to control men's minds through modern devices. He alters brain patterns through back-masking records in which a satanic message can be heard. Although the conscious mind cannot comprehend backward messages, the subconscious mind can. Psychologists also found that if you place a single frame with a message every twenty frames in a film, the conscious mind cannot pick it up. But the subconscious mind can. In one experiment reported by Vance Packard in his book *Hidden Persuaders*, a single frame showing popcorn was placed in every twentieth frame. Sales of popcorn increased tremendously.

Although the federal government outlawed such hidden persuaders, evidence of such techniques persist. Pictures of some sordid scene or satanic message can be cleverly hidden in commercial ads. The conscious mind cannot pick it up, but the subconscious mind does. Television, radio, movies, and magazines present demonic messages every day. Violence, murder, perversion, and rebellion are standard fare. One Hollywood writer claims that three ingredients must be present in any successful movie: violence, rebellion, and sex. Children's cartoons constantly depict violence and make demons appear as friends or cute harmless things. Movies such as Star Wars and E. T. remain among the most popular, and their ideas are derived from Buddhism and the demonic realm.

Evidences of Mind Control

The spirit of Mind Control often brings headaches. It also brings unteachableness, hardness of mind, stubbornness, depression, unbelief, and unwillingness. Some people go through years of teaching but never learn anything. They still cling to old ideas and beliefs no matter what. They have been brainwashed and cannot get rid of their ways of thinking, even when proven erroneous by the Word of God. A kind of stupor exists where the victim cannot see reality or truth. They see things only through tinted glasses, so to speak. It brings narrowed vision, and the person cannot seem to understand the things of God.

Deliverance from Mind Control

Since the spirit of Mind Control is related to Leviathan (Pride) and appears in the shape of a giant squid, you need to bind up Leviathan and cut off the cords. Bind up Orion in the heavenlies also. Dry up the waters of the enemy. A deliverance session against mind control usually takes time. Each tentacle must be withdrawn from the person's mind. I've found that coals of fire from the altar of God often works. In other cases, the Holy Spirit shows me bands about the head and body of the person. I ask God to send angels to cut them off or dissolve the bands.

Witchcraft steals fragments from the souls of people (Ezek. 13:18–22). Verse 22 says: "*Because with lies ye have made the heart of the righteous sad, whom I have not made sad.*" Ask God to send as many angels as are necessary to retrieve the fragments of that person's soul which have been stolen, return them, and restore their proper order and to quicken and bring them back to life. Ask God to heal the mind and the memories.

Occult Mind Control is related to Witchcraft and the ruling spirit of Witchcraft is Babylon or Jezebel. You need to bind up Witchcraft and Jezebel in the heavenlies. I list some of the spirits used by the ruling spirit of Mind Control below:

Bands on Head	Headaches	Mental Disease
Unbelief	Doubt	Faithlessness
Giant Squid	Tentacles	Chanting
Meditation	Strange Religions	Mantras
Hopelessness	Tiredness	Oppression
Exhaustion	Unconsciousness	Mental Blank

In addition to the above strongmen, you need to recognize that Mind Control opens the gates to other clusters of spirits. For instance, if a person falls for the belief that she brought about the death of her sister, spirits such as Fear of Discovery, Self-Accusation, Condemnation, Self-Hate, Suicide, and Shame, also come in. You need to cast them out along with these other possible spirits:

Stupidity	Error	Hypnosis
Cults	Blindness	Darkness
Compulsiveness	Strange Habits	Strange Clothes
False Holy Spirit	Strange Voices	Misunderstanding
Confusion	Depression	Passivity of Mind
Misleading Spirit	Disagreement	Passivity of Body
Disorderliness	Distraction	Disconcertedness
Untidiness	Bewilderment	

The Word of God

The Word of God is Truth and it brings faith (Rom. 10:17). We need to have our minds constantly cleansed with the washing water of the Word. It is the Word that drives out deception and lies. We stand on the Word because it is Truth.

It is extremely difficult for Satan to deceive you if you have the Word of God buried in your heart. That is why we measure everything against the Word of God. If the idea or thought is contrary to the Word of God, it is not from God; it is a lie.

Step by step, we need to be cleansed of all unrighteousness, all lies, and all things not of God. It is still the engrafted Word that is able to save our souls.

Chapter Sixteen

The Spirit of Murder and Violence

The spirit of Murder and Violence will become very powerful in the end times. Not a single day goes by without murders and wars going on somewhere in the world. This spirit encourages killing and destruction between men, tribes, and nations. Wars and conflicts continue to disturb peace on planet earth and will become more intense with time. Reports indicate that as many as fifty to sixty wars take place each year in various parts of the world. When the number of wars drops to the mid-twenties, it represents relative peace.

Every year, thousands of humans are maimed for life or murdered. People slaughter other people for no apparent reason. Hardly a day goes by without a report of some grisly murder. Some killings are so horrible, one knows that only Satan could be the instigator of such cruelty.

The earliest account of murder and violence took place when Cain slew Abel. Genesis 4:8 says, *"and it came to pass, when they were in the field, that Cain rose up against Abel his brother, and slew him."* Since Cain, murder and violence have risen continually between and among men and their brothers. What mankind does to one another in the area of murder cannot come from anywhere but the very pit of hell.

In the end times, men will go the way of Cain, killing one another. Jude 11 reads, *"Woe unto them! for they have gone in the way of Cain."*

An increase in wars, violence, and murders is a sign of the end times. Christians will be martyred by the millions (Rev. 6:9; 13:7). It's not difficult to visualize a world where Christians are hunted down and killed systematically. In Matthew 24:9, Jesus says, *"Then shall they deliver you up to be afflicted, and shall kill you: and ye shall be hated of all nations for my name's sake."* The stage for mass murder is already set and in place. It is just a matter of time.

The spirit of Babylon, or Jezebel, controls Murder and Violence. In Revelation 18:24, the Word says, *"in her was found the blood of prophets, and of saints, and of all that were slain upon the earth."* That spirit uses Unforgiveness, Jealousy, Anger, Pride, Bitterness, Hatred, Hostility, Covetousness, Mind Control, and other lesser spirits to set the stage for Murder and Violence. The Babylonian system is a worldwide system based on desire for power and wealth (Nah. 3:9). It finds its base or strength in pride. The pride of Egypt, during the time of the prophet, Nahum and the riches of Ethiopia were dominating forces. They still are today. National pride and desire for riches on a world-wide basis lead to war and conquest. The word "war" actually describes an effort by one group to use violence and/or murder upon another group, in contrast to one individual murdering others.

In the end times, Murder and Violence shall become all powerful. Nation will rise up against nation, and kingdom against kingdom (Matt. 24:7). Even now, people seem to be on killing sprees. Atrocities in Africa continue. Organized groups slaughter whole tribes of Africans. Often, these victims belong to the same nation as the perpetrators. At one point it will appear that a solution for wars and violence has been discovered—one-world government. It is a remedy worse than the disease it attempts to heal. It is only a pipe dream.

The spirit of Death, of course, is a close country cousin. Death does not necessarily come through violence or the agency of another person. Death also works through disease or accident. Murder, however, works through another human.

Jesus said in John 8:44 of Satan, *"He was a murderer from the beginning, and abode not in the truth."* The very character of Satan smacks of murder. From the beginning, Satan has been murdering humans. Whenever one human or a group of human beings murder another, Satan takes delight. Stories of murder and war abound in the Bible and in the legend and history of every country on the face of the earth. During the end times, Satan shall be cast down to earth, and he will be furious (Rev. 12:8–9, 13). Because of this, Satan will go to make war against the church.

*And the dragon was wroth with the woman,
and went to make war with the remnant of her
seed, which keep the commandments of God,
and have the testimony of Jesus Christ.*

(Rev. 12:17)

In Revelation 13:7, the beast shall make war against the saints. *"And it was given unto him to make war with the saints, and to overcome them: and power was given him over all kindreds, and tongues, and nations."* War represents organized violence and murder condoned by governments or leaders.

Trying to Kill Jesus

When Jesus walked the earth, Satan constantly stirred up the people to incite them to murder Jesus.

*Then Herod, when he saw that he was mocked
of the wise men, was exceeding wroth, and
sent forth, and slew all the children that were
in Bethlehem, and in all the coasts thereof,
from two years old and under, according to
the time which he had diligently inquired of
the wise men.* (Matt. 2:16)

In another incident, Satan put the idea to kill Jesus into the minds of the Pharisees, but it wasn't His time so Jesus escaped through the crowd (John 7:30). On numerous occasions, the Pharisees sought to kill Jesus because He taught things not in agreement with their doctrines.

And therefore did the Jews persecute Jesus, and sought to slay him, because he had done these things on the sabbath day. But Jesus answered them, My Father worketh hitherto, and I work. Therefore the Jews sought the more to kill him. (John 5:16–18)

In John 7:1, the Bible reports, "*After these things Jesus walked in Galilee: for he would not walk in Jewry, because the Jews sought to kill him.*" In the end, when the time arrived, Jesus allowed Himself to be killed on the cross. The spirit of Murder and Violence worked constantly to kill Jesus. Satan continues to use that spirit and plans to kill all Christians in the end times. He plans to rile up the governments, nations, and people. In their frenzy, they will commit murder, just as he riled up the Pharisees when Jesus walked the earth.

Killing the Prophets

The power of Murder can also be observed in the fact that Satan provided for the murder of every prophet sent by God to the Jews. Isaiah, Jeremiah, Ezekiel, John the Baptist, and many other prophets died at the hands of enemies or their own people. Jesus bewailed the fact that Jerusalem killed off the prophets sent by God.

In the End

During the end times, the spirit of Murder and Violence will run even more rampant. Matthew

24:6–7 says, "*see that ye be not troubled: for all these things must come to pass, but the end it not yet. For nation shall rise up against nation, and kingdom against kingdom.*" We will see murder and violence like never before in the history of the world.

Matthew 24:9 says, "*Then shall they deliver you up to be afflicted, and shall kill you: and ye shall be hated of all nations for my name's sake.*" Christians as a group shall be targeted by Satan for wholesale slaughter.

Revelation 6:9–11 talks about the souls of those who were slain for the Word of God and the testimony that they held. Multitudes of Christians will be beheaded during tribulations.

In deliverance, the fact that one has not killed anyone does not necessarily indicate the presence or absence of the spirit of Murder and Violence. The spirit could be working in a person slowly through unforgiveness and bitterness. A person may not have physically committed murder, but the spirit hides in his heart. That is why Jesus said if a man hates his brother, he has already murdered him in his heart. Hatred and Unforgiveness are gatekeepers who invite the spirit of Murder into a person's life.

Abortion

In most of the cases of abortion that I've worked on, the spirit of Murder and Violence manifested itself. Abortion involves the spirits of Murder as well as Death. The over twenty-four million abortions a year worldwide attests to the success of this spirit. That's twenty-four million murders a year that take place in the area of infants alone. Who knows how many more die as a result of isolated murders and wars? In an earlier paragraph, I mentioned that Jezebel controls the spirit of Murder. As Satan's present Commander in Chief, this vile spirit controls all seven ruling spirits, including Murder. Revelation 18:24 is talking about this present day and age.

Suicide

Suicide is self-murder and usually manifests itself as a serpent. In one particular case, I was talking to a young woman who was distressed about her husband leaving her. As we spoke, the Holy Spirit suddenly said, "Suicide." I looked at the woman and asked, "Did you try to commit suicide?" She immediately broke down and started to sob. She then admitted that the night before she was about to take a handful of sleeping pills, but at the last moment she threw them down the toilet. I said, "Suicide, you come out in the name of Jesus!" The young lady immediately started to cough and choke. She fell on the floor, started to move like a serpent, and her tongue began to flick from side to side. The demon spoke in a hissing voice, "I'm not coming out." As I looked down upon the woman, I saw the muscles along her backbone ripple as if the snake had wound itself around her backbone. He soon came out.

In every case of Unforgiveness and Hatred, there is a potential for the spirit of Murder and the spirit of Violence to be present also. Suicide works in conjunction with Unforgiveness of Self and Self-Hatred.

Over Entire Nations

Murder and Violence can enslave entire nations and peoples. I believe that Nazi Germany was under the control of this ugly spirit. Even today, certain areas of the world are bound by Murder and Violence. Certain peoples, because of their cultural histories, are more prone to manifest this particular spirit. In some South Pacific islands, many violent spirits manifest in one particular race almost every time I give deliverance—mass or individual. All the while, people of different ethnic backgrounds in the same audience remain calm and sedate.

Binding Up Murder and Violence

Murder, being a ruling spirit, must first be bound in the heavenlies, and its cords must be cut off and cast away. Cast out Murder and Violence in the same manner as with other spirits. You need to clean out the entire nest of spirits of Bitterness, Anger, Hostility, Hatred, Unforgiveness, and related spirits. In some cases, you need to get specific: Hatred for Father, Mother, Men, Women, et cetera.

Behind Murder is the spirit of Pride. You may have to dig Pride out first. Many a murder has been committed because of pride.

In every case of despondency, consider Suicide as a possible spirit. In cases of anger, especially with people who are child abusers, wife beaters, and wall smashers, you need to handle Murder and Violence.

The jurisdictions of the seven ruling princes overlap. If you place the tops of seven pyramids side by side, their bases will overlap greatly. Ruling spirits have joint use of many spirits. Listed below are some of the spirits used by Murder and Violence:

Suicide	Anger	Hostility
Unforgiveness	Bitterness	Long Memory
Revenge	Martial Arts	Ki or Chi
Cruelty	Torture	Beater
Hate	Estrangement	Loner
Animosity	Resentment	No Love
Obnoxious	Brutality	No Mercy
Jealousy	Envy	Holding a Grudge
Self-Centeredness	Betrayal	Disloyalty
Greed	Covetousness	Pride
Hurt	Abortion	Stillborn
Miscarriage	Rebellion	Fear

Chapter Seventeen

The Spirits of
Death and Hades

Death is a spirit; so is Hades. Some deliverance writers lump the two together as one spirit. Death and Hades work so closely together that some view them as one. My experience indicates that Death and Hades are two distinct and separate spirits. The Bible often speaks of Death by itself and sometimes refers to Hades by itself.

Death is an Enemy

God considers the spirit of Death to be an enemy. First Corinthians 15:25–26 says, *"For he must reign, till he hath put all enemies under his feet. The last enemy that shall be destroyed is death."* Death should never be considered a friend. Christians often talk of death as a welcome friend that makes it possible for them to be with Christ. In truth, Jesus came so that we need never die.

The Bible also calls death the waster (Isa. 54:16) and the destroyer (Exod. 12:23). Revelation 6:8 says, "*And I looked, and behold a pale horse: and his name that sat on him was Death, and Hell followed with him.*" Again, Revelation 20:14 says, "*And death and hell were cast into the lake of fire.*" I believe that Death acts as the executioner that brings about the demise of an individual, and then Hades or Hell takes charge of the unbeliever. Believers go to heaven escorted by angels. Those destined to hell find themselves in the hands of the spirit of Hades who controls all unfortunate souls who never made it to heaven.

Death, being an enemy and an evil spirit, falls under the control of the believer. Luke 10:19 says, "*Behold, I give unto you power to tread on serpents and scorpions, and over all the power of the enemy: and nothing shall by any means hurt you.*"

A few years ago, I spoke to a group of women about spiritual warfare and the spirit of Death for several weeks. The women, all born-again Christians, listened on with deep interest. I taught them how to bind up the strongman in the heavenlies and how to rebuke and call out the spirit of Death.

Several months went by until one day I received a telephone call from one of the women. It seems that the husband of another woman in my class died while pulling weeds in his back yard. The wife could not be found since she left to go shopping in the morning. The neighbors called an ambulance and a fire truck with a resuscitator. The neighbors also summoned a physician who declared the man dead.

Twenty minutes later, the wife returned. When the doctor told her of her husband's death, she refused to accept it. She started walking around the house binding up the spirit of Death in the heavenlies and every strongman she could think of. She then grabbed her husband's cold body, rebuked Death, and commanded it to leave. His body started to warm up again; he opened his eyes and came back to life. He is still alive and well today. The ambulance and fire-truck personnel and the physician accepted Jesus Christ as their Savior that day.

A year or so ago, one of the women in our church prayed over a woman who had dropped dead in the parking lot of her store. She was disappointed when the woman failed to respond. The ambulance came, and the attendants declared her dead and proceeded to ask questions of the by-standers. After twenty minutes, they slowly drove away. Two months later, the woman appeared in her store to thank her. It turned out that the ambulance workers had deposited her in the hospital morgue, and the resident doctor examined her and signed a death certificate. When he walked out of the room, she came back to life. She had a slight loss of memory and paralysis of the right arm, but after two months of rehabilitation, she was back to normal.

We have the keys to hell and death.

Abortions

In cases of abortion, the spirits of Death and Murder often linger on and torment the woman. In one encounter, while I prayed for a woman who went through an abortion, the woman turned cold in her body. She started to shiver. I rebuked Death and commanded it to leave. The woman coughed and dry-heaved and suddenly became warm again. The spirit of Death left. Since then, I've been involved in a number of similar cases where Death surfaced during deliverance. Death can also torment men or other people who somehow consented to an abortion. It could be someone who arranged for the abortion, paid for it, recommended it, or assented to it. Such people often feel a dark cloud or a foreboding presence over them.

In many cases, the spirit of Death manifests during healing sessions. The spirit of Infirmity and the spirit of Death work together. Death sometimes works over a long period of time, as in a long sickness, or suddenly, as in an accident. Before the healing can take place, the spirit of Death often needs to be bound up and cast out. Of course, the Holy Spirit is the deliverer, and in many healings He just moves sovereignly in the area of miracles. A person with the gifts can heal without ever mentioning the spirit of Death.

Waters of Death

The River Jordan represents a type and shadow of death. The Hebrew nation had to cross over the Jordan to get to the promised land. Greek legends call it the River Styx. Myths claim that the boatman, Charon, ferried those that die over the river to get to paradise or whatever their destiny. Those unable to pay for the boat trip must wander aimlessly upon the face of the earth—a cruel fate. On the other side, if one lived a meritorious life, he went to paradise; if not, he went to Tartarus. The Bible calls Tartarus the deepest pit of hell. Orientals burn paper money, clothing, and even cars in the belief that they could be taken by the dead into the next life. They put coins in the mouths of the dead in the belief that the dead have to pay the boatman to get across the River of Death.

The Word of God indicates that when the ark of the covenant went ahead and the people kept their eyes on the ark, the River Jordan rolled back and the people went over on dry land (Josh. 3:16; 5:1). It was a type and shadow of heavenly things to come. One day, God's elect will walk into the promised land without tasting death. They will keep their eyes steadfast on Jesus Christ, the Ark of the Covenant. God, of course, has complete power over waters (Job 26:5–10).

The Bible frequently equates death to water or shadows. The "shadow of death" is an expression often found in Scripture. A shadow, of course, brings darkness to mind. People who claim to have died and come back to life often report traveling through darkness or a dark tunnel. On the other hand, God and life are associated with light (Job 12:22; 18:5; 30:28; Ps. 27:1; 36:9; 43:3; 56:13; Prov. 4:18; Isa. 9:2). Jesus is the light of the world (Matt. 4:16; Luke 1:78–79; John 1:4–5, 7–9; 3:19; 8:12; 9:5; Eph. 5:14). The Bible also mentions gates of Death. Therefore, in deliverance, I often ask God to dry up the waters of Death, to bring His light to shine upon Death, and to tear down the gates of Death.

The Blood Defeats Death

When Moses led the Hebrew nation out of Egypt, God instructed Moses to have the people kill a perfect lamb and sprinkle its blood on the side posts and lintel of the door. At midnight, the destroyer passed through and killed the first born of every creature. When the destroyer saw the blood on the doorway, he passed over. God did not allow him to enter that house. Thus, the spirit of Death must pass over when he sees the blood of Jesus on the door.

During deliverance, I claim the blood of God's Lamb upon the doorway of the person being delivered. "I sprinkle the blood of Jesus all over the gates to his body and soul." Death must pass over.

The Worms

People sometimes see worms in the spirit.

And upon a set day Herod, arrayed in royal apparel, sat upon his throne, and made an oration unto them. And the people gave a shout, saying, It is the voice of a god, and not of a man. And immediately the angel of the Lord smote him, because he gave not God the glory: and he was eaten of worms, and gave up the ghost. (Acts 12:21–23)

This passage is strange because Herod was still alive when the worms began eating him, and then he gave up the ghost or died. However, in the spirit it is not strange because the worms of Death begin eating one's flesh and soul even before physical death actually takes place. Such is the case of one doomed to hell.

One afternoon, a pastor dropped into my office. He had just come back from visiting a sick person in a nearby hospital. The sick person was a well-known musician who had suffered a stroke. The pastor was perplexed at something that happened at the hospital. Because the musician was popular, the pastor couldn't get into the room. As he sat in the hallway praying, he suddenly looked up and had a vision of a stream of worms moving through the walls and into the room of the musician. As he spoke to me of his experience, the Holy Spirit brought the story of Herod to mind. I opened my Bible and was surprised to find that the Scriptures said that the worms ate him and then he gave up the ghost.

In the natural, a person normally dies first, and then the worms consume his flesh. I told the pastor, that the young musician would die because he didn't give God the glory. My pastor friend replied, "That's true, he always gave credit to his Hawaiian gods." The young musician died at five P.M. that day.

In deliverance, ask God to turn back the worms. Dry them up and turn back the worms of death with fire from heaven.

Spirit of Hades

The Spirit of Hades, or Hell, takes charge of the souls of those who die and do not go to heaven.

In *Visions Beyond the Veil*, the authors served as missionaries in China in the early 1900s. They ran an orphanage for Chinese street children. One day during morning prayer, the Spirit of God fell upon the orphanage, and many of the children spoke in tongues and saw heaven in visions. Groups of children entered the gates of heaven and saw Christian friends and family who had died before. They even saw people in heaven who had died without their knowledge and whose deaths were confirmed later after they came out of their visions. When they returned from their heavenly visions, their reports matched each other's in every way.

God also allowed them to see many things on earth and things to come in the end times. The children saw demons wandering the earth and even saw demons surrounding unbelievers on their death beds. When the unbelievers died, the demons put chains around their necks and dragged their spirits down to hell.

In the book *Return from Tomorrow* by a Dr. Richie, the Christian brother related how he died of a flu at age nineteen while at boot camp during World War Two. His spirit left his body, and he found himself being escorted by someone he later knew as Christ. He testifies that during that time he saw many disembodied spirits wandering the earth. This time of wandering tormented the dead because the lusts they failed to control during life increased ten times. If they loved alcohol, their need for alcohol increased tenfold. If they loved sex, their sexual lust increased tenfold. They could not satisfy their lusts in the spirit realm, and the lusts became torment. The spirits with a lust for alcohol hung around bars trying to lap up drinks but to no avail.

Those with sexual lust kept trying to satisfy their lust but could do nothing. At the end of his experience in the spirit, Dr. Richie returned to the camp hospital, re-entered his body, and came back to life to the total shock of the doctors attending.

Set or Seth

I ministered to a young lady who experienced many scary things—hands grabbing her at night, shadows moving across her room, and voices talking or laughing at her. We prayed for revelation on her problem because the nightly spectral visitors perplexed us. Then a member of the church dreamt about Alice one night. In the dream, he saw Alice standing in a long single file line with many other people with a sad countenance on their faces. They seemed to be moving in a line that entered a cave leading into the earth. As the dreamer entered the cave, he saw a large figure of a man with the head of an animal—a wolf or jackal. Chains around their necks joined the people in the line to one another. As the people approached the man, they would stop, and the man placed masks over their heads. When Alice stepped up before him, the man also placed a luminous brick on her shoulder. The dream ended at that point.

The church member thought that the dream reminded him of some mining operation. As the church member related the dream to me, I recognized the scene from ancient Egyptian hieroglyphics that depicted the dead and the underworld. The man with the head of a jackal actually represented the god of the dead or the underworld, Hades. The Egyptians called this "god" Set or Seth. The luminous brick reminded me of the door to the world of the wandering dead. In myths, disembodied spirits live in a nether world of semi-gloom, where it is cold, wet, and swamp-like, where they wander aimlessly, tormented by the cold and loneliness of the spirit dimension in which they are confined.

The following Sunday, I related the dream to Alice and gave her my interpretation that the spirit of Seth or Hades was the one tormenting her. Even as we spoke, something inside of her quivered with fear. That evening, Seth came out.

Hell's Territory

Hell or hades also represents a territory or kingdom. The words "Sheol" and "Hades" are not found in the King James version. The word "Hell" is used. However, other translations do use the words "Sheol" and "Hades."

Hades has different levels. Deuteronomy 32:22 speaks of the *"lowest hell."* Therefore, there must be higher levels of hell. This is also mentioned in Psalm 86:13. The Bible usually refers to hell as being "down" or "below" the earth (Ezek. 32:27; Matt. 11:23; Luke 10:15; Job 11:8; Prov. 9:18). Hades means "the unseen," "place of departed souls," "grave," and "hell." Death is also associated with depths and downward elevation (Prov. 5:5). The deepest part of hades is called Tartarus.

We also know that there is fire in Hell (Matt. 5:22) and that Hell has gates (Matt. 16:18). Other words associated with hell include "sorrows of hell," "pains of hell," "destruction," and "the pit."

Deliverance from Hades

It is not so much deliverance from Hades itself that occupies us, but rather, the familiar spirits that Hades sends to torment. Often, tracing one's ancestors or family tree to uncover murderers, abortions, miscarriages, stillborn infants, abnormal patterns of behavior, strange ancestors, or ancestors who practiced strange religions helps to expose open gates through which the enemy can enter.

Chapter Eighteen

The Hawaiian Religion

I hope that this chapter will help Christians understand and counteract recent attempts by native peoples to go back to ancient demon religions. What applies to the Hawaiian people may well apply to American Indians and other indigenous groups around the world.

A Christian Problem

The American Indians, Hawaiians, Maoris, Tahitians, and other indigenous groups are going back to ancient animistic religions in an attempt to rediscover their roots. It is a direct satanic attack on Christianity. If Christians merely sit back and fail to defend the kingdom of God, Satan will have his way.

Hawaiian Demon-Gods Today

The current wave of Hawaiian restoration recently induced the local board of education to require Hawaiian studies at the elementary school level. These studies portray the ancient Hawaiians as a noble race with kind and protective gods. Unfortunately, the resurgence also resulted in restoring the worship of Hawaiian demon-gods. There is definitely a romanticizing of Hawaiian religion and culture, and a rejection of Christianity. Many television programs present a beautiful picture of ancient Hawaiian culture and religion by glorifying Pele, Kihawahine, and other demon-gods. Hula festivals and contests create a sense of pride in culture, and hula "halaus" (troupes) flourish today. These hulas originated from dances to demon deities and constitute an integral part of ancient Hawaiian religious rites.

Today, organizations dedicate themselves to restoring Hawaiian heiaus (temples) on every island, and even Christian churches volunteer to restore and care for heiaus in the misguided belief that this shows love. They also joined together to ask forgiveness for not respecting the gods and culture of the Hawaiians. Can you imagine churches apologizing to demons and recognizing their right to rule over the Hawaiians?

In one sense, Hawaiian culture never completely perished. Modern kahunas (priests) traditionally bless buildings, and legislative sessions and surfing meets are traditionally opened by a kahuna blowing conch shells and chanting. The general desire for ceremony and pageantry is satisfied by colorful ancient Hawaiian rituals to demon gods. The local people have always appreciated Hawaiian food, hula dancing, music, and stories. Hawaiian musicians and artists constantly promote the ideas that their Hawaiian gods bring them success, and that there is power or "manna" that every person of Hawaiian ancestry can tap into.

Kahuna—Pastors

Hawaiian Christian leaders even fall into the trap of adopting Hawaiian ways to entice people into church. They use Hawaiian chants and proclaim that the Hawaiian gods Lono, Kane, or Kanaloa, represent Jesus or Jehovah, and that bowing to them is bowing to Jesus. They employ the paraphernalia of kahuna: gourds, calabashes, ti leaves, salt, malos (loin cloths), kahilis (feather standards), leis, and hulas. They recite Hawaiian chants and substitute Kane for Jesus. They dance the hula in church and sprinkle water and salt as they walk up the aisle. Kahunas claim to be Christian ministers that have existed since the beginning. They carry and quote the Bible but worship Hawaiian deities.

A Curse on the Hawaiian Race

Hawaiians can take pride in their culture and knowledge of nature. Hawaiian mariners possessed an uncanny knowledge of the stars, tides, and ocean. Their navigational knowledge astounds the modern sailor, and their natural friendliness and caring for others should be copied by everyone. Hawaiians are a beautiful people—both physically and culturally. Their intelligence is unquestioned. You can find Hawaiians in medicine, education, law, engineering, and business.

Nevertheless, the Hawaiians have not been blessed as a race. Fewer than 3,000 pure-blooded Hawaiians remain today. At one time, over 400,000 lived on the islands. In the mid-1800s, a new race of part-Hawaiians emerged. Today, there are over 200,000 part-Hawaiians, the vast majority of whom have less than one-half Hawaiian blood. In fact, the famed Kamehameha Schools recently readjusted admission standards to accept students with one-eighth Hawaiian blood. The Hawaiian race is at the brink of extinction.

Those who are part-Hawaiians (we continue to call them Hawaiians) fare very poorly as a group. They constitute 80%–85% of the Oahu Correctional Facility (a State prison) population, and part-Hawaiians remain vastly underrepresented among the professions. Most Hawaiians are blue-collar workers. Worse still, an overabundance of Hawaiians live on welfare. They constitute one of the lowest ethnic groups in both education and yearly per capita income.

The Missionaries—A Hawaiian Viewpoint

The rallying cry of the Hawaiian sovereignty movement is a direct attack on Christianity. A large number of very vocal sovereignty movement leaders have rewritten Hawaiian history to blame all the ills of the Hawaiian people on the introduction of Christianity to the islands. The missionaries who came to Hawaii are now accused of being the sole cause of the downfall and destruction of the Hawaiian religion, culture, and people.

The Truth

The good life that Hawaiians lived is fictional. The *alii* (chiefs) owned all the land and kicked out the commoners at will. The common people were utterly oppressed. It was death for a commoner to remain standing at mention of the king's name, even in a song, or when the king's food, water, or clothing were carried past. They could not even touch the shadow of an alii or his house. In the presence of alii, they had to crawl. The alii did not work. They took two-thirds of the food produced by the commoners. The commoners lived in fear of the *kahunas* (priests) who could choose anyone for a human sacrifice. Human sacrifice was required for just about everything, from the building of a canoe to the building of an alii's house. The alii and kahunas controlled everything by placing taboos or *kapus* on all the good foods and activities such as surfing. The women especially were oppressed by many different taboos. They were second-rate subjects.

In 1779, Captain Cook estimated that there were 400,000 pure Hawaiians. When Captain Vancouver visited the Islands in 1792, he noted a marked decrease in population which he attributed to devastating wars among the people. In 1823, there were only 142,000, and the 1830 census indicated 130,313. The year 1853 counted 70,036; 1884 showed 40,014; and 1896 indicated 30,019 pure Hawaiians. In short, the population was already on a decline at the time the Hawaiians became exposed to civilization.

Anthropologists concluded that two contributing factors already existed at the time of Captain Cook's exploration. First was the very low birth rate. Adults cared very little about raising children because they were too busy with their constant sexual pursuits which started at an early age. They avoided pregnancy and practiced widespread infanticide. About two-thirds of all babies, especially females, were killed. The second factor was constant warfare. The death rate exceeded the birth rate.

Although many Hawaiians died because of poor immunity against various diseases, other races such as the Tongans, Samoans, Tahitians, and Marquesans bounced back after two generations. Disease alone cannot be blamed.

They Destroyed Their Own Religion

In 1819, the Hawaiian rulers announced a repudiation of the Hawaiian religion of kapus and animistic gods. When the missionaries arrived in 1820, there was a religious void. After landing, they were greatly opposed by the white traders who were particularly cruel to the natives. The white traders tormented the missionaries because of their stand against alcohol, prostitution, and sexual promiscuity. White traders and adventurers controlled the king and even used arms against the missionaries. In 1825, five years after their arrival, only ten Hawaiians had been baptized. In 1832, of all the Hawaiian Islands, only 577 claimed to be Christian. Claims that the Christians stole the Hawaiians' religion and culture are historically false, but often spoken of, nonetheless. How could 577 Christians take away the Hawaiians' religion and steal their culture during a period of twelve years?

Liberation of Commoners

The missionaries saw the cruel oppression over the common people and campaigned to guide them through a turbulent time when the alii were desperately trying to adjust to western ways and the common people had no rights. The missionaries were able to break the taboos that kept the commoners in bondage and release women from virtual slavery. Queen Kaahumanu, a wife of King Kamehameha, embraced Christianity, and later Queen Kapiolani and other royalty became steadfast Christians.

The Great Mahele in 1849, which made lands available to the commoners, was seen as absolutely necessary in order to release the common people from the power of the alii. The missionaries were especially active to see that the natives were not imposed upon by unscrupulous whites. As a result, over 50% of the commoners owned their own homes. Over 780,000 acres were owned by natives and 1,000,000 by whites. Later, the natives began selling their lands for piddling amounts to sharp Yankee traders so that over a thirty years span of time, the native holdings dwindled from 46% to only 6%. Today, Hawaiians claim the missionaries stole their land.

The missionaries, in their attempts to help the natives survive the onslaught of western greed, organized over one hundred schools, many hospitals, and churches. Unfortunately, their efforts are now seen as cruel and oppressive, so Christianity has taken the blame for devastating the Hawaiians. Nothing could be further from the truth. Granted, many missionary descendants joined with Yankee traders in buying large amounts of acreage, and ended up controlling the economy. However, it is obvious that even without the missionary descendants, it was inevitable that Yankee traders along with the great influx of other races into the Islands would have had the same overall effect. The Hawaiians were simply not ready, nor could they combat the tremendous social, religious, and cultural changes which sudden exposure to civilization brought. It was a tidal wave that could not be stopped.

The above facts were much documented by publications by anthropologists and writers prior to 1910. See especially, *Christus Redemptor, An Outline Study of the Island World of the Pacific,* 1906, by Helen Barrett Montgomery, the MacMillan Company. Early accounts of Hawaiian history differ sharply from modern versions.

Christians Are Not Blameless

Christian missionaries came to Hawaii in 1820 and stayed for thirty years. Many returned to New England to retire and live out the rest of their lives. Hawaiian cconversion to Christianity was actually largely the result of the Charles Finney revival that took place in the mid- to late-1800s. By 1890, almost 95% of the Hawaiian race was saved. Meanwhile, the missionary descendants were not quite as zealous and Christlike as their predecessors. They were more interested in material growth than spiritual results.

A Christian cabinet overthrew the monarchy around 1893. The ruler, Queen Lilioukalani, served on the same church board with some who arrested her. One group of Christians openly warred against another group of Christians for control of the Sandwich Islands.

By the 1950's, Christian haoles (white men) owned 90% of the major businesses in Hawaii. All of the telephone, electric, gas, water, bus, trust, and shipping companies, banks, and every major business belonged to missionary descendants and their partners. These descendants were haughty and arrogant, and they treated Hawaiians and other minorities like slaves. Meanwhile, Hawaiians began to understand the tremendous evils done to their race. They were stripped of their lands—fences now ran from mountain to ocean so they could no longer fish, hunt, or grow crops on land they formerly had free access to. They could not understand the rough treatment to which they were being subjected. They were a friendly and loving race, but now had no money in a world where money was king. In addition, disease ravaged the Hawaiians because of a nonexistent immune system created by centuries of no disease. Even the common cold decimated entire villages, and up until the 1960's, tuberculosis, leprosy, and small pox plagued thousands of Hawaiians. Foreign merchants and sailors introduced venereal diseases and many other pestilences.

Sometimes epidemics would kill Hawaiians by the hundreds in one week. It is reported that out of hopelessness many Hawaiians simply lay down to die.

During this period, the white Christian community did virtually nothing to help the hapless Hawaiians. Many missionary descendants lived luxuriously in southern plantation style homes, complete with Roman bath-houses, servants, dalmatians, lawns of three to five acres, horses, and all the accoutrements of excessive wealth. They enjoyed the cheap labor of many minorities and ruled with an iron hand. Racial discrimination continued well into the 1960's.

When the U.S. Congress fully accepted Hawaii as a territory in 1920, they worked out an agreement intended to alleviate the plight of native Hawaiians. Congress ruled that over 140,000 acres of land must be turned over to the Hawaiians as homestead lands for rehabilitation and farming. However, once more, white Christians controlled the Land Commission. They proceeded to give virtually all the arable lands to the white men and left the Hawaiians the rocky, salt infested, or inaccessible lands. For instance, 45,000 acres on the top of the remote Mauna Loa volcano were handed over to the Hawaiian Homes Commission. Thousands of acres were given on remote Molokai, famous for its lack of water. Thousands of acres of land in Waianae and Waimanalo were turned over to the Hawaiians because of their salt-poisoned soil. Papakolea, next to Punchbowl crater, was mostly cliffs and blue rock. In many cases, there simply was no water available. Ironically, the plantations, always ready to make a deal, leased many of those lands for one dollar an acre a year and later proceeded to build irrigation systems which now provide rich returns. The haoles also later purchased most of the beachfront properties at bargain prices from the Hawaiians—a keg of whiskey, a case of beer. To the starving Hawaiians beachfront properties were worthless.

Even the Bishop Estate, the famed public trust created by Bernice Pauahi Bishop to care for the children of Hawaii (interpreted as those of Hawaiian ancestry), was administered solely by haoles. There were many abuses. It wasn't until the 1970's that a part-Hawaiian was finally appointed to serve as Trustee.

The state government itself has shown only token interest in the Hawaiians' plight, and its performance is lamentable—always too late with too little. The Hawaiian Homes Commission has been frustrated almost every year by a lack of funds and interest by legislators, administrators, and the public. It takes a Hawaiian a lifetime to obtain a home site. Some have waited for forty years with still no results.

The non-Hawaiian community is lukewarm at best, and lip service remains the most common response to the Hawaiians' problems. No matter what the part-Hawaiians do, if rekindling the Hawaiian culture is the only thing to come out of the renewed emphasis on Hawaiiana, even the part-Hawaiians are doomed as a race. Sovereignty will not solve that problem.

Breaking the Curses

Christian leaders should band together to ask forgiveness of the Hawaiian people for the sins of our Christian forefathers so that the Hawaiian people can be set free from the curses of unforgiveness (Matt. 18:35).

We cannot sit idly by while the Hawaiian people fall into hell. Helping the Hawaiian people live a better life or become an independent nation is secondary to leading them to Jesus Christ. Should we not be like Peter who said in Acts 3:6, "*Silver and gold have I none; but such as I have give I thee*"? Helping the Hawaiians in the area of financial welfare is good, but setting them free from curses is even better. Once again, there is a spiritual void which the Hawaiian people fill with demon worship. Shame on us.

In order to deliver Hawaiians from their demon gods, you need to have an understanding of Hawaiian religion. In order to help the people in your area, you need to know something about their native religion. The similarities to other native, animistic religions found in Polynesia, the South Pacific, Africa, and other areas is so striking that a study of Hawaiian religion will, no doubt, help you deal with those religions.

Hawaiian Religion

Through phonetic similarities in the native language, anthropologists trace Hawaiian culture back to Egypt and the Semitic nations of the Middle East.

Interestingly, Egypt and Hawaii both had a matri-
archal society. Women inherited the family wealth,
and the men married their sisters in order to keep
the wealth. Incest became widespread among the
ruling families of both Egypt and Hawaii. Because
of the belief that "manna" or supernatural power
was passed down the family line, the Hawaiian alii
(chiefs) married their own sisters and other close
relatives.

Three Classes of Hawaiians

There were three major classes in Hawaiian
society: (1) The "alii" or ruling class of warriors
and kings, (2) the "kahuna" or priestly class, and
(3) the commoners. There were other minor classes
such as the slaves, untouchables, and legendary
menehunes (little people). Class lines were clearly
defined. The aliis were larger in stature than the
others and ruled with iron fists. In fact, anthropologists from Yale at first thought that the alii
and kahuna people were a separate race from the
commoners. When aliis went among commoners,
the commoners were required to prostrate themselves so that aliis could walk upon their bodies.
The aliis spent most of their time practicing martial arts and plotting war strategies. The commoners were required to provide the aliis with food and
serve them hand and foot.

There are almost no descendants of the aliis left
in Hawaii today, yet most Hawaiians see themselves
in the role of aliis and not commoners. They think
of themselves as superior to others.

Kahunas

The kahunas, or priests, provided spiritual guidance. However, the word "kahuna" also applied to anyone trained in a special skill. There were kahuna experts for canoe making, healing, house making, and for many other kinds of skills. However, the most feared kahunas were the ones who dealt in sorcery. Sorcery kahunas were the only kahunas that could be female. Hawaiians feared sorcery kahunas for their ability to cause the death of people without touching them.

Kahunas served as counselors to the alii who consulted them on every important occasion. In times of war, the kahunas became very important. Through them the chiefs could learn from the gods when and how to attack the enemy and whether they would be successful. Success and failure depended on appealing to the gods and obeying the instructions of the kahuna. The only possibility of defeat was if the adversary's manna proved stronger.

The common people feared the kahunas that served the "Ku" gods. Ku required human sacrifices, and the kahunas possessed absolute power to determine who became one. Although some sacrifices came out of the untouchable class of people or from enemy warriors, commoners often served as sacrifices. Pigs, dogs, and fish substituted for humans on less important occasions.

Akua

The Hawaiians worshipped several classes of gods. At the top were the creation gods called *akua*.

Next came the *aumakua* or family deities, some reputed to be as powerful as akua. Other spirit beings included the *unihipili* or spirits of the deceased converted into helpers by a *kahu* or keeper who cultivated these spirits by feeding and chanting to them. A *kupua* was a person who was born with special deity powers and was said to be the offspring of a god and a human.

The akua class was comprised of four male gods: Kane, Kanaloa, Lono, and Ku. Kane was primarily the god of agriculture, rain, and growth. Kanaloa was the god of the bottom of the sea, wild vegetation, and the dead. Lono was god of vegetation, trees, and the sun.

Ku was the god of warfare. Ku is noted for his desire for human flesh. He comes in many forms, one of which is the hawk. In the spirit realm, he is huge and dressed in a warrior's outfit complete with helmet, cape, malo, and spear. People have seen him in visions. Interestingly, deliverance ministries on the West Coast and in Canada claim that the ruling spirit up and down the continent is the hawk god. Eskimos revere him and give him the top position on their totem poles. Even in the ancient Aztec, Inca, and Toltec religions, the eagle or hawk spirit reigned supreme. North American Indians also worship the hawk or eagle, especially the tribes along the West Coast and in Arizona, Utah, and other western states.

Human Sacrifice

As already mentioned, Ku demanded human sacrifices. The first three captives in battle ended up sacrificed to Ku. There were many "Ku" gods which the alii adopted as personal gods.

Human sacrifice was by three different methods: strangling, drowning, and bashing. Interestingly, ancient European demon cults used the same three methods of human sacrifice. You may recall that the Aztecs, Toltecs, and Incas also required human sacrifice. Demons are the same all over the world. They love to be worshipped through human sacrifice, which gives them power.

Although modern Hawaiians claim otherwise, the obsession for ultimate power will lead a person to human sacrifice. Already there are reports of animals being sacrificed in remote woodland areas. Hawaiian gods, of course, are all demonic in nature. A person involved in Hawaiian religion gradually drifts toward the supernatural or psychic side of worship. Many Hawaiians speak of kahuna power with pride because of the "good" things it can do. For centuries people have been involved in different forms of witchcraft with the finest of human intentions. Some claim that healing power enables them to help the sick; others love to predict the future in order to help others; many desire to elevate themselves spiritually. Power corrupts even the finest of intentions. At that point, human sacrifice is just around the corner.

Aumakua

Hawaiians worship *aumakua* as family or personal gods or guardian spirits. Idols, chants, and customs are passed down the family line. More than one family can worship the same aumakua, and any individual can adopt a particular aumakua as his or her personal "guardian" deity. The more popular aumakua include Pele (the fire or volcano goddess), Kihawahine (the lizard goddess), Kamapua'a (the pig-man god), the plover, owl, *mo-o* (lizard), shark, and dog. Interestingly, aumakua such as Pele and Kihawahine are reputed to be vengeful deities who just as quickly killed their worshippers as helped them, but the desire for power blinds men.

Pele is a very cruel deity. Her normal form is an ugly old hag dressed in filthy rags which scarcely cover the filth and nakedness of her body. She has bloodshot eyes, a fiendish countenance, and her touch turns men to stone. She is a jealous and vindictive monster with a terrible temper and brings eye and other diseases. But, the Hawaiian people and visitors from around the world have romanticized her and only see her as a benevolent, beautiful, young lady full of love and caring for the Hawaiian people. In legend, she is a lustful creature who devours her lovers. She takes her anger out on the people by erupting and burning their villages with lava.

Obviously, with Pele you need to ask God to send floods of water to put out her fires. We treat her in much the same fashion as we handle Jezebel or Babylon the great. Her ally is Kamapua'a, the pig god who controls the ocean's water. Therefore, you need to dry up the waters also. It sounds paradoxical, but it isn't. The waters of death are not the same as the living waters of the Holy Spirit. Neither are the fires of hell the same as the fires of the Holy Spirit.

Kihawahine, a thirty-five foot lizard (actually a dragon) lives in inland swamps. She is a *mo-o*, a lizard goddess. She can also appear as a mermaid with long flowing tresses. Modern Hawaiians portray her as a beautiful, young lady, but in reality she is a vindictive, cruel monster. She brings diseases such as smallpox, leprosy, sores, cancer, colds, and the flu.

Hiiaka i ka poli o Pele is the younger sister of Pele. She slaughters many lesser gods and destroys Hawaiians. Kahunas pray to this spirit to kill people. She is the patron goddess of hula.

Kapo is another younger sister of Pele. She is revolting and impure. I treat Hiiaka, Kihawahine, and Kapo as I would any other foul spirit and cast them out using the blood of Jesus.

Kamapua'a is half-pig, half-man. He is very powerful, and legends claim that he almost defeated and destroyed Pele. He has bristles on his back and a snout for a nose and loves to root around the forests. He controls the surface waters of the sea. He desired to have Pele as his lover, but when she laughed and called him ugly, Kamapua'a retaliated by sending torrents of water from the sea to put out the fires of Pele. The gods intervened, however, when they realized that Kamapua'a would destroy the fires which were needed on earth. They convinced Pele to accept Kamapua'a as a lover and in time, Pele came to adore Kamapua'a as a sexual partner.

Kamapua'a is the Hawaiian god of sexual lust. People with this spirit are constantly tormented by sexual fantasies, lust, and insatiable desires. They think of sex almost all the time and situations that feed their lust arise constantly. In addition to lust, this spirit represents sexual promiscuity, fornication, adultery, perversion, homosexuality, and masturbation. It cannot stand against the blood of Jesus. Since Kamapua'a uses the sea water, you need to dry it up, using Jeremiah 50:38, 51:36, and similar verses.

Unihipili

A *kahu* or keeper entices spirits to do his bidding by feeding and soothing them. When an infant dies, a kahu would persuade the parents to let him have the body. He then takes the remains and buries it in the forest or throws it into the ocean after much chanting. If he worshipped the shark god, for instance, the kahu would chant to the shark god and place the remains in the ocean. He would return to chant and throw food in the same spot in the ocean daily. Eventually, he would observe a baby shark swimming in the area. It is said that the spirit of the baby is now in the shark. The kahu then continues feeding the shark and chanting daily. Eventually, he entices the spirit to leave the shark and come to the kahu for feeding. Besides food and chanting, the kahu would introduce *awa*, or liquor made from ti plant roots. He would spray awa into the air with his mouth. Once the spirit becomes addicted to awa, it starts to do the bidding of the kahu.

If the kahu wanted to kill someone, he would send the *unihipili* out to entice the soul of the victim to come to the kahu. Hawaiians believed that a man possessed two souls, one of which wandered around while the man slept. If this wandering soul were led to the kahu, the kahu would either strangle it to death or seal it in a special gourd. Within three days, the victim would die. (For a more detailed description of Hawaiian religion and history, see Martha Beckwith's *Hawaiian Mythology*, Gavan Daws' *Shoals of Time*, and Lawrence H. Fuch's *Hawaii Pono*.)

Disembodied Spirits

Local lore is filled with ghost stories. It is said that disembodied spirits haunt houses and areas all over the islands. There are multitudes of stories about ghostly encounters and night marchers. Of course, native Hawaiians (I am not of Hawaiian ancestry) and locals are not concerned about whether these spirits are demons or ghosts. In addition, native temples called *heiaus* dot the islands. These heiaus (high places) are said to harbor demons and disembodied spirits. Hawaiian spirits are said to inhabit rocks, so people who bring rocks into their homes risk the possibility of unwanted nocturnal visitors.

Local residents often hire kahunas to cleanse buildings. They use more powerful demons to chase out weaker demons. Witch doctors and shamans have been doing that for centuries all around the world, not just in Hawaii. A person is "cured" of a bad back by a kahuna, only to die of heart disease a few years later. The Bad Back demon is chased out by the Heart Disease demon who takes over.

Deliverance from Hawaiian Demons

Objects

Hawaiian objects can also bring curses to a house. Ancient musical instruments or implements, such as the ipo (gourd), bamboo, or pebbles, although relatively modern in manufacture, could house Hawaiian demons. Kahunas often talk to demons in rocks by clicking pebbles. Once these objects are disposed off, the problems disappear. Homosexuality is one such problem. Hawaiians are cursed with homosexuality through the worship of Pele, a female deity. Males in the house become "mahu" (effeminate), and females become lesbians. The normal "tita" or tough, masculine Hawaiian woman may not necessarily be lesbian, but many are.

Jewelry and body ornaments can be demon possessed, especially if passed down the family line. Necklaces, ankle and wrist feather bands, even tapa cloth can represent legal grounds for the enemy. Sometimes, it is not so much the type of object or material, but the fact that some ancestor chanted over it or dedicated it to some aumakua. A tapa cloth may be just a tapa cloth. Another tapa cloth may have been prayed over so that "manna" would remain in the cloth.

Carvings of tiki gods are also within that realm. Authentic tiki carvings all had a certain design, and most carvers or artists are not so discerning as to create an exact replica. Nevertheless, the intent to create a tiki god may be sufficient to allow entry by demons.

Family Worship

Many Hawaiian families worship "aumakua" or deities. This practice is worldwide in the sense that many families worship some special deity that they consider peculiar to their family. Even Jacob's father-in-law worshipped family deities. Modern Hawaiians often don't admit it, but they talk to their aumakua and put food at designated places and chant or sing to their deities. Many feel that it is harmless and simply a show of respect. Many talk to dead aunts, grandfathers, brothers, and spouses. Such worship brings curses on family members. Children have hideous diseases such as weeping eye, venereal lesions, club feet, and boils. There is a price to pay for sinful worship.

Often, even Christians will be tormented by Hawaiian curses and diseases, although they do not practice the kahuna religion themselves. In one case, a woman's grandfather worshipped Hiiaka, one of Pele's sisters. The women was tormented. As we prayed for her, I saw a white blackboard, and on it a hand wrote the word, "Hiiaka." I didn't even know what the word meant. As I related what I saw, the demon manifested and came out. It was exposed. Upon questioning, the woman revealed that Hiiaka was one of her family's aumakuas.

In another case, a girl was tormented by temper tantrums and fear. As we prayed for her, I saw a shark in a vision. Upon questioning, she confessed that the shark was her family deity and that she had a painting of the shark god in her bedroom.

Needless to say, the painting gave the demons the right to stay and torment.

In still another case, a Christian brother related how God had given him a gift of healing. He collected and grew many different kinds of plants and herbs in his yard. When friends came to him for various ailments, he knew instinctively which herbs to give them, and they were invariably healed. As he was speaking, the Holy Spirit gave me one word, "kahuna." I asked the person if he had Hawaiian blood (he didn't look it). He answered "Yes." He revealed that his grandfather on his mother's side came from a long line of healing kahunas. The man was a large man and could have picked me up with one hand and tossed me through my seventh story window. When the person he came with asked me to pray for the man, I replied that I would ask God to bless him, but I would not pray for deliverance.

As I laid hands on him, he started to wail and shout, "I see him! I see him!" "What do you see?" I asked. "A man with a malo and white hair. I see a *heiau* with *tapa* and *kahilis* and an altar. He's waving at me and telling me not to pray." As we continued to pray, I commanded the spirit to leave, and he came out. Afterwards, the brother was so weak that it took him fifteen minutes to get up and leave. God had taken away his physical strength to prevent him from harming us. Needless to say, his healing powers disappeared. Even tongue-speaking Christians, like this brother, can have demons. If you're part-Hawaiian, your spirits could have come down the family line.

This brother had never worshipped his grandfather or any other Hawaiian demon, but nevertheless, he was indwelt by the kahuna ancestor. Many families believe in beneficent ancestors who hang around to "help out" other family members. In fact, kahunas pass down *manna* (power) by breathing into a child's or descendant's mouth or by chanting and rubbing a tattoo designed for that purpose. A family tattoo is placed on a child from infancy for the purpose of receiving the family spirits and the family manna. Hawaiians call this manna supernatural power, but manna is none other than the power of evil spirits.

Witchcraft as we know it in America or Europe uses an identical system. Witches know that their supernatural manna or power comes from demons. The stronger the demon is, the more forcible the manna. Rebecca Brown explains this beautifully in her two books, *He Came to Set the Captives Free*, and *Prepare for War*.

Infestation through Trespass

Many individuals become infested with Hawaiian demons because they intentionally trespass on *heiaus*. In one case, a Puerto Rican woman from New York attended a class in Hawaiiana at Chaminade College. The entire class slept in a heiau overnight as part of a class project. Nothing unusual happened except that she remembered sleeping on a stone slab which later turned out to be a human sacrifice altar. She became infested with Hawaiian demons.

In another case, a young man went on a vacation to the Big Island where a bus tour took him and his family to a *heiau* (temple/altar site) in the area where Captain Cook landed. They suffered from strange nocturnal visits for years before God showed them the source.

One visitor from the mainland, the son of a friend of mine, was over six feet six inches tall. He didn't believe in Hawaiian superstitions. He went to the same heiau where Captain Cook landed at Kealakekua, Hawaii. While taking photos, he stood on the altar. By the time the tour bus returned to his hotel, he couldn't stand up. His back was so painful, his wife and friends had to carry him. Unfortunately, there was no Christian present and he took the advice of the Hawaiian bartender who advised him to take some pork and ti leaf and place it on the altar and apologize. With much difficulty, he returned in a rented car, planted the sacrifices on the altar and apologized. Almost immediately, the pain left. According to his father, the man was so frightened that he cut his vacation short and returned to the mainland.

Kahuna Curses

As mentioned earlier, Hawaiian kahuna sorcerers were the most feared kahunas in Hawaii. Their existence is attested to by numerous stories. Kahunas who could kill people without coming into contact with their victims existed up until modern times. The island of Molokai was known for its sorcerers who lived and trained there and who had the ability to kill people. Even today, many aspiring young kahunas go to the island of Molokai to retrieve some of the lost arts and secrets. They live in the forests and attempt to get in touch with some ancient aumakua or gods that will be beneficial to them.

Heiaus in the Body

Demons greatly desire worship and will create a place of worship to themselves within the person. A Hawaiian demon will build a heiau; a Buddhist spirit will build an altar with incense box, candles, food bowls, and other items that appear in a Buddhist temple.

Hawaiian demons will build a rock enclosure, a platform replete with altar, kahili, bone enclosure, hut, and tiki carvings. As you destroy them by asking God to send angels and fires from heaven to demolish the heiau and tear down all rock walls, the demons will scream, "No, No, stop it." As you destroy the heiau, or soon thereafter, the demons will leave.

Animism

For the most part, the worship of various animal and nature forms saturates the entire Hawaiian religion. The same form of religion permeated Babylonian and Egyptian religions and can be found all over the world, but especially in the South Pacific. Most demonic religions share the same foundation.

Hawaiian Pride

Pride in being Hawaiian and also the spirit of King Kamehameha have surfaced during deliverance. Pride prevents us from really receiving and giving God's love.

The King Kamehameha spirit is a macho spirit that men adopt to paint themselves as noble, strong natives. They work on body building and all the activities that bring the image of super-maleness such as football and surfing. If not, they assume an obnoxious tough guy personality. That spirit is not unique to Hawaiians, just predominant. All races have their own version, and it is based on insecurity and bitterness.

In Summary

Satan has launched an all-out attack to destroy the Hawaiian people in retaliation for their turning to God. Once again fellow Christians are turning their backs on Hawaiian Christians in their hour of need. We need to recognize this insidious attack and get into the battle on behalf of the Hawaiian people. Sovereignty is not our topic to support or not support. It is our willingness to stop Satan that is the issue.

Chapter Nineteen

A Tsunami Coming

The greatest revival and harvest of souls the world has ever known is coming soon. It will also be the last. In the midst of this revival will come persecution and eventually all-out extermination of the saints. Satan's beast is going to wage war against the saints and overcome them (Dan. 7:21; Matt. 24:9; Rev. 13:7). It will be dangerous to be a Christian.

Satan is not afraid of revival. He has survived every revival and remains the prince of this world to this day. But this one is going to be different. It will involve direct confrontation against the kingdom of darkness through spiritual warfare and deliverance. Satan wants to stop this revival and destroy all Christians before his kingdom is annihilated. Soon, he will launch an all out attack on the body of Christ.

We are going to have to stand and fight against Satan's hordes of demons. That's why God is raising up an army of saints today. It's going to be the greatest army of men and women that ever walked the earth (Joel 2:11). On the other hand, multitudes of Christians will fall away from the faith when they become disillusioned and are unprepared (2 Thess. 2:3). Some saints will be martyred and a remnant will survive the tribulations ahead, but most will fall (Matt. 24:22; Rev. 6:9, 11; 12:11, 17).

Big Changes Coming Soon

In 1994, during a span of one week, three people approached me about interpreting their dreams. In all three cases, they saw old buildings about to be inundated by a huge tidal wave or *tsunami*. There was nothing they could do but hang on. The wave hit the buildings and swept most people and structures away. Some survivors were seen hanging onto the concrete foundations. In the few buildings that remained (one in each dream), the insides were swept or washed clean. Nothing remained. In one dream, only a few very young Christians around eight to ten years old survived. In another dream, the dreamer walked up the street after the wave subsided and saw a group of church people dressed alike standing around. Their faces were ashen and their eyes glazed. One woman held a bunch of green onions and kept repeating, "I have to go home to cook."

My interpretation was this: The old buildings represent the church which has been around for about 2,000 years. The tsunami represents either a flood of evil spirits about to descend upon the church or a purging of the body of Christ or both. In any case, the church is about to be cleaned up. Many saints who still insist on clinging to foundational doctrines only will find themselves out on the street, spiritually dead. Some will not notice what is going on because they are too concerned about the things of life.

Nine months later (two months before writing this chapter), a young prophet invited me to lunch. He asked me about a dream he just had. It was identical with the other three—the same old buildings, tsunami, and washing away of everything. God is confirming once more that a great purging will take place soon.

The coming changes will shake the church by its very foundations. Stubborn churches that refuse to move into spiritual maturity will not survive the trials and purgings. What you did yesterday will not be good enough for today, and what you do today will not be good enough for tomorrow. The doctrines and level of spiritual growth that were sufficient for your parents will not carry you through what is about to happen.

The Old Will Give Way to the New

"Behold, the days come, saith the LORD, that the plowman shall overtake the reaper, and the treader of grapes him that soweth seed" (Amos 9:13). The latter will come before the former, the young before the old, stale saints. I too came out of a conventional, foundational church. When I was born-again, I readily discarded stiff, unworkable doctrines that claim that there are no such things as demons, speaking in tongues, and miracles. I was so hungry for truth that I devoured the Bible and plunged into

deliverance with everything I had. I became an elder within eight months. Many who had been Christians for twenty or thirty years resisted me. Today, they too have been left behind. Those who refuse to move on will be swept away (Heb. 6:1–2).

The finest hour of the church is fast approaching. This is the chosen generation that will fulfill all prophecy and that will take the kingdoms of this world back from Satan and hand them over to God (1 Corinthians 15:24). They will destroy all of God's enemies, and the last enemy to be destroyed is death (v. 26). There is going to be a battle for the ages, and in the end, the true church of God is going to win!

Yes, deliverance and spiritual warfare are not everything, but without knowledge and experience, a saint will have little chance in the war about to descend upon the church. You can't read your way through a fight. You need to get into the battle. You have a deadly enemy bent on destroying you. Either join the battle and learn to fight, or perish!

God's Army

When the body of Christ becomes the militant church that Jesus originally came to establish, Satan is going to fall like lightning from heaven (Luke 10:18).

In a number of places where I have taught, people have seen a huge angel standing to the left and back of me. Angels sometimes walk into the room and form a circle around us. Some carry suits of armor to put upon the students. Often, angels surround me on the platform while I teach deliverance. I'm not trying to convince you about how great I am. I'm just a man. I'm trying to tell you how serious God is about His army.

Whenever I return from the mission field after teaching on deliverance and spiritual warfare, letters from places such as Fiji, Sarawak, Singapore, Malaysia, and the Philippines filter in, telling of miraculous healings, deliverances, raisings of the dead, and revivals starting. As the people war against the demonic kingdom, they see angelic hosts fighting alongside them. Many see white horses standing outside or coming to the church or Bible college (Rev. 19:11, 14). Others have visions of the church members or students dressed in battle fatigues. They are all in God's army.

God is calling His sanctified ones, His mighty ones (Isa. 13:3). His army is starting to march forward. The trumpet is blowing. Can you hear it? (Joel 1:2). It's time for you to answer His call!

Appendix A

We thank William D. Banks of Impact Christian Books and Frank and Ida Mae Hammond for their kind permission to reprint the diagram that appears on the following pages.

The diagram originally appeared in *Pigs in the Parlor*, ©1973, published by Impact Christian Books, Inc., 332 Leffingwell #101, Kirkwood, MO 63122.

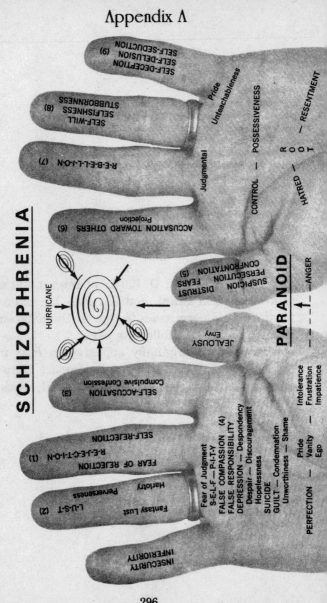

SCHIZOPHRENIA

(9) SELF-DECEPTION
SELF-DELUSION
SELF-SEDUCTION

(8) SELF-WILL
SELFISHNESS
STUBBORNNESS

(7) R-E-B-E-L-L-I-O-N

(6) ACCUSATION TOWARD OTHERS
Projection

Pride
Unteachableness

Judgmental

CONTROL — POSSESSIVENESS

HATRED — RESENTMENT

R
O
O
T

PARANOID

(5) CONFRONTATION
PERSECUTION
FEARS
SUSPICION
DISTRUST

ANGER

JEALOUSY
Envy

HURRICANE

(3) SELF-ACCUSATION
Compulsive Confession

(1) R-E-J-E-C-T-I-O-N
SELF-REJECTION
FEAR OF REJECTION

(2) L-U-S-T
Fantasy Lust
Harlotry
Perverseness

INSECURITY
INFERIORITY

Fear of Judgment
S-E-L-F — P-I-T-Y
(4) FALSE COMPASSION
FALSE RESPONSIBILITY
DEPRESSION — Despondency
Despair — Discouragement
Hopelessness
SUICIDE
GUILT — Condemnation
Unworthiness — Shame

Intolerance
Frustration
Impatience

Pride
Vanity
Ego

PERFECTION — PERFECTION

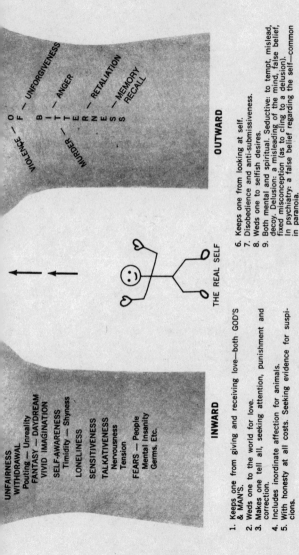

THE REAL SELF

OUTWARD

VIOLENCE — O — UNFORGIVENESS
F
B — ANGER
I
T
T
MURDER — E — RETALIATION
R
N — MEMORY
E — RECALL
S
S

6. Keeps one from looking at self.
7. Disobedience and anti-submissiveness.
8. Weds one to selfish desires.
9. Both mental and spiritual. Seductive: to tempt, mislead, decoy. Delusion: a misleading of the mind, false belief, fixed misconception (as to cling to a delusion). In psychiatry: a false belief regarding the self—common in paranoia.

INWARD

UNFAIRNESS
WITHDRAWAL
Pouting — Unreality
FANTASY — DAYDREAM
VIVID IMAGINATION
SELF-AWARENESS
Timidity — Shyness
LONELINESS
SENSITIVENESS
TALKATIVENESS
Nervousness
Tension
FEARS — People
Mental Insanity
Germs, Etc.

1. Keeps one from giving and receiving love—both GOD'S & MAN'S.
2. Weds one to the world for love.
3. Makes one tell all, seeking attention, punishment and correction.
4. Includes inordinate affection for animals.
5. With honesty at all costs. Seeking evidence for suspicions.

References

Baker, H. A. *Visions Beyond the Veil*. Springdale, PA: Whitaker House, 1973.

Beckwith, Martha. *Hawaiian Mythology*. Honolulu, HI: University of Hawaii Press, 1985.

Brown, Rebecca, M.D. *He Came to Set the Captives Free*. Springdale, PA: Whitaker House, 1986.

————. *Prepare for War*. Springdale, PA: Whitaker House, 1987.

Cho, Dr. Paul Yonggi. *The Fourth Dimension*. South Plainfield, NJ: Bridge, 1983.

Davis, Gavan. *Shoal of Time, a History of the Hawaiian Islands*. Honolulu, HI: University of Hawaii Press, 1974.

DeHaan, M. R. *The Chemistry of the Blood*. Grand Rapids, MI: Zondervan, 1943.

Fuchs, Lawrence H. *Hawaii Pono*. Honolulu, HI: Bess, 1961.

Grubb, Norman. *Rees Howells Intercessor*. Washington, PA: Christian Literature Crusade, 1952.

Halley, Henry H. *Halley's Bible Handbook*. Grand Rapids, MI: Zondervan, 1965.

Hammond, Frank and Ida Mae. *Pigs in the Parlor*. Kirkwood, MO: Impact Christian Books, 1973.

Hunt, Dave, and McMahon, T. A. *The Seduction of Christianity*. Eugene, OR: Harvest House, 1985.

Lamb, Bob. *The Overcoming Blood*. Springdale, PA: Whitaker House, 1993.

McAull, Dr. Kenneth. *Healing the Family Tree,* ninth edition. London: Sheldon, 1986.

Michaelson, Johanna. *The Beautiful Side of Evil*. Eugene, OR: Harvest House, 1982.

Montgomery, Helen Barrett. *Christus Redemptor, An Outline Study of the Island World of the Pacific.* New York: MacMillan, 1907.

Nee, Watchman. *Love Not the World.* Wheaton, IL: Tyndale House, 1987.

————. *The Spirit of Wisdom and Revelation.* New York: Christian Fellowship Publishers, 1980.

Packard, Vance. *Hidden Persuaders.* New York: D. McKay Company, 1957.

Penn-Lewis, Jessie. *War on the Saints,* unabridged ninth edition. New York: Thomas E. Lowe, 1981.

Pittman, Howard O. *Demons An Eyewitness Account.* Foxworth, MS: Philadelphia Publishing House.

————. *Placebo.* Foxworth, MS: Philadelphia Publishing House.

Prince, Derek. *Blessing or Curse, You Can Choose!* Tarrytown, NY: Fleming Revell:, 1990.

Ritchie, George G., M.D. *Return from Tomorrow.* Grand Rapids, MI: Zondervan, 1978.

Whyte, Maxwell H. A. *The Power of the Blood.* Springdale, PA: Whitaker House, 1973.

Worley, Win. *Eradicating the Hosts of Hell.* Lansing, IL: Win Worley, 1980.

ANOTHER POWERFUL Book

from Whitaker House

Demons and Deliverance
H. A. Maxwell Whyte

Satanic activity continues to increase at an explosive
rate. Maxwell Whyte provides practical answers to
the most frequently asked questions about demons.
Discover how you have the authority to defeat
oppression, addiction, sickness, mental problems,
and unexplainable behavior with lasting results.

ISBN: 0-88368-216-8 • Trade • 192 pages

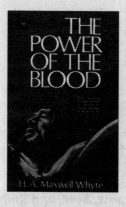